W9-BUX-076

THE LIVING MOMENT

Also by Jeffrey Hart

Political Writers of Eighteenth-Century England

Viscount Bolingbroke, Tory Humanist

When the Going Was Good! American Life in the Fifties

From This Moment On: America in 1940

Acts of Recovery: Essays on Culture and Politics

Smiling Through the Cultural Catastrophe: Toward the Revival of Higher Education

The Making of the American Conservative Mind

THE LIVING MOMENT

Modernism in a Broken World

Modernism in a Broken World

JEFFREY HART

NORTHWESTERN UNIVERSITY PRESS
EVANSTON, ILLINOIS

Northwestern University Press
www.nupress.northwestern.edu

Copyright © 2012 by Northwestern University Press. Published 2012. All rights reserved.

An earlier version of chapter 1, "Robert Frost and T. S. Eliot: Modernisms," was first published in the *Sewanee Review* 114, no. 4 (Fall 2006). Copyright © 2006 by Jeffrey Hart.

Printed in the United States of America

10 9 8 7 6 5 4 3 2 1

Library of Congress Cataloging-in-Publication Data

Hart, Jeffrey Peter, 1930–
   The living moment : modernism in a broken world / Jeffrey Hart.
      p. cm.
   ISBN 978-0-8101-2821-7 (pbk. : alk. paper)
   1. Modernism (Literature)—History and criticism. 2. Literature, Modern—20th century—History and criticism. I. Title.
PN56.M54H37 2012
809.9112—dc23

2012005927

♾ The paper used in this publication meets the minimum requirements of the American National Standard for Information Sciences—Permanence of Paper for Printed Library Materials, ANSI Z39.48-1992.

To Nancy,

who makes it all possible

An odd secret excitement, a strange need,
To be there with words when the heartbeat happened.
                    —Mark Van Doren

Speech is the body of the Spirit.
                    —Eugen Rosenstock-Huessy

CONTENTS

During the first part of the nineteenth century, literature—both poetry and prose—was able to assume a coherent culture that the writer shared with the reader. For complex reasons this situation gradually ceased to exist, and the First World War put an emphatic end to the assumptions of the nineteenth century. In *A Broken World: 1919–1939*, Raymond James Sontag quoted Gabriel Marcel, who in 1933 felt he was living in a broken world, "like a watch with a broken spring; in appearance nothing was changed and everything was in place, but put the watch to the ear, and one heard nothing."

In *The First World War*, John Keegan made the connection between that apocalyptic war and the decades that constituted the middle of the twentieth century. The great Russian poet Anna Akhmatova called the middle of the twentieth the "time of troubles," surely an understatement. Keegan describes the connection between the "Great War" and the "time of troubles":

> On 18 September 1922, Adolf Hitler, the demobilised front fighter, threw down a challenge to defeated Germany that he would realise seventeen years later: "It cannot be that two million Germans should have fallen in vain . . . No, we do not pardon, we demand—vengeance!"
>
> The monuments to the vengeance he took stand throughout the continent he devastated, in the reconstructed centres of his own German cities, flattened by the strategic bombing campaign that he provoked, and of those—Leningrad, Stalingrad, Warsaw, Rotterdam, London—that he himself laid waste. The derelict fortifications of the Atlantic Wall, built in the vain hope of holding his enemies at bay, are monuments to his desire for vengeance; so, too, are the decaying hutments of Auschwitz and the remnants of the obliterated extermination camps at Sobibor, Belzec and Treblinka. A child's shoe in the Polish dust, a scrap of rusting barbed wire, a residue of pulverised bone near the spot where the gas chambers worked, these are as much relics of the First as of the Second World War. They have their antecedents in the scraps of barbed wire that litter the fields where the trenches ran, filling the French air with the

smell of rust on a damp morning, in the mildewed military leather
a visitor finds under a hedgerow, in the verdigrised brass of a badge
or button, corroded clips of ammunition and pockmarked shards
of shell. They have their antecedents also in the anonymous remains
still upturned today by farmers ploughing the bloodsoaked soil of
the Somme—"I stop work at once. I have a great respect for your
English dead"—just as the barely viewable film of bodies being
heaped into the mass graves at Belsen in 1945 has its antecedents
in the blurred footage of French soldiers stacking the cordwood of
their dead comrades after the Second Battle of Champagne in 1915.
The First World War inaugurated the manufacture of mass death
that the Second brought to a pitiless consummation.

In *A Broken World,* Sontag dates the brokenness as beginning in 1919,
which indeed was the year it became manifest. But the nineteenth-century
consensus had begun to break down long before, first in France and then
in England, where the middle class had greater cultural authority. It is
important to understand this social background, because it created the
problems modernists address. The modernist response was various and
complicated but often profound, and the great modernist works are of
lasting value. All of this will require attention if the reader is to understand the sources and the achievements of this important development.

T. S. Eliot's *Waste Land* appeared in 1922, its structure fragmentary,
and the poem full of fragments of Western culture. Near the end of
The Waste Land is the phrase "These fragments I have shored against
my ruins," which reverberated all through the literature of the 1920s
and became the banner of modernism. In fact, however, the challenges
addressed by modernism had been present long before 1922, as modern
thought in various forms as well as social stresses called in question the
assumptions of the nineteenth century.

The Living Moment will address the erosion of nineteenth-century
assumptions in France and substantially later in England, and also the
important responses modernist writers made to the cultural crises that
resulted. The issues involved are complex and difficult and so often is the
modernist response. The reader here can expect some hard work as well
as the pleasure of exploration and discovery.

THE LIVING MOMENT

The Living Moment in a Broken World

Things fall apart; the centre cannot hold;
Mere anarchy is loosed upon the world.
                    —W. B. Yeats, "The Second Coming"

"An odd secret excitement, a strange need,/To be there with words when the heartbeat happened." That was the poet Mark Van Doren on the experience of writing poetry, the words reflecting something not entirely rational, and perhaps even a physical experience. For the attentive reader poetry makes things happen in the mind; it changes the reader, however subtly. And this is true of many novels.

Modernism in both poetry and the novel was usually characterized by heightened originality of form, often by difficulty, and by the centrality of the extraordinary moment with which to organize experience. The difficulty repelled many readers, but it had the effect of forcing attentive readers to engage with the work of literature in a cooperative way to create an island of coherence. Moreover, many modernist works transcended their period and contributed permanently valuable insights.

It is important for the reader to understand the social and historical circumstances that created the cultural crisis that modernism addressed, a sense in advanced circles that the nineteenth-century European order had become false and that we were living in a broken cultural world. Such modernism will be the focus of this book.

The principal reason why England had an authoritative Victorian culture may be found in a surprising place, Samuel Richardson's six-volume novel *Clarissa* (1746). Hardly anyone reads *Clarissa* nowadays, even in an abridged edition. Most readers would be surprised to learn that this enormous and almost forgotten mid-eighteenth-century novel was a work with latent revolutionary implications.

Clarissa is also an example of how reading can imperialize the reader, as is Rousseau's *Julie; or, The New Eloise* (1761), heavily influenced by *Clarissa*. Both of these enormous novels can take days to read. And this is part of their accumulating power. Their readers must have had the time to delve into the shades of thought and feeling explored by these epistolary narratives. I want to emphasize, however, that *Clarissa* possesses potentially revolutionary implications, as Clarissa Harlowe, daughter of a wealthy middle-class family, defends her independence against the sexually predatory Sir Richard Lovelace. She is attracted to Lovelace but insists on her own terms. Her defense of her virginity is a defense of her integrity and, inferentially, an assertion of middle-class rights. Lovelace, after hundreds of pages, finally drugs her, rapes her, and for that pays with his life in a duel with Colonel Morden, her avenging relative. Notice, this duel must take place in France, not England. Half a century later in France the guillotine would reenact this scenario on a very large scale. As Samuel Johnson said to Boswell, "If you were to read Richardson for the story, your impatience would be so much fretted that you would hang yourself. But you must read him for the sentiment. . . . There is more knowledge of the heart in one letter of Richardson's [*Clarissa*] than in all *Tom Jones*."

There were more politics as well in *Clarissa*. British aristocrats had to reform their manners—no more dueling, swagger, swearing, spitting on the floor; they had to marry the wealthy Clarissas instead of chasing them and raping them. And they gradually agreed to meet the wealthy commoners on the middle ground of the new social ideal of the gentleman, the wealthy commoners even acquiring landed estates. In *The Spectator* (1711–14), Addison and Steele popularized the style—urbane, mildly witty, condemning with a smile: as the Tory Alexander Pope, Addison's enemy, said of him, "willing to wound and yet afraid to strike." *The Spectator* provided the smattering of knowledge suitable to a gentleman. Of course James Gatz wanted to become an English gentleman known as Jay Gatsby, even an "Oxford man." The gentleman tertium quid ameliorated social hostilities in England, as England, unlike France, solved its problems one at a time. In 1649, with the execution of Charles I, absolute monarchy ended. In 1688 with the Glorious Revolution, a parliamentary overthrow of James II, the supremacy of parliament was consolidated. None of this happened in France, where, indeed, the revolutionary tradition remained strong at least until recently, that is, with the uprising of 1968. *Political consolidation and the ideal of the gentleman created the solid Victorian era in England.* The "decadents"—Wilde, Beardsley, Dowson, Pater—were culturally marginalized.

As Dowson joked about the decadents, "absinthe makes the tart grow fonder."

Modernism as a rebellion against an order felt to be false therefore appeared much earlier in France, the bourgeoisie lacking cultural authority, and vulnerable. Paris built the Eiffel Tower on the Champ-de-Mars for the 1889 centennial of the Revolution. Designed by the engineers Maurice Koechlin and Émile Nouguier, its iron construction clashed with the surrounding architecture of Paris and was denounced by traditionalists as a pissoir. In France, modernist art announced its presence dramatically with the 1886 Exhibition of the Independents, and Verlaine, Rimbaud, Laforgue, and Mallarmé were clustered around 1873 to 1885. Rimbaud's *Une Saison en enfer* (*A Season in Hell*) appeared in 1873, asserting the *truth of disorder* against the *false order* of the nineteenth century, his "derangement of all the senses" (*dérèglement de tous les sens*) inviting comparison with Eliot's much later *Waste Land* (1922). In 1913 the Armory Show introduced modernist art to America, with French contributions dominant. When modernism did appear strongly in England, two of its most prominent figures were Americans, Ezra Pound and T. S. Eliot, along with James Joyce, an Irishman.

In 1915 Pound persuaded, or forced, Harriet Monroe to publish "The Love Song of J. Alfred Prufrock" in her magazine *Poetry*, even though she did not understand it. Hart Crane had to explicate in a famous letter to Monroe the very difficult "At Melville's Tomb" before she would publish it. "Prufrock" was part of a new revolution. It begins:

> Let us go then, you and I,
> When the evening is spread out against the sky
> Like a patient etherized upon a table.

That third line, sharply dissonant, comes as a surprise.

We are in the presence of Prufrock's unconscious. Prufrock wants to "go," as that lyrical opening couplet indicates, but pulls back toward a jumble of thoughts connected with surgery, ether, fear, a desire for oblivion.

Clearly this is a broken metaphor, the word *Like* failing to establish a connection with "When the evening is spread out against the sky." This could not have come from Tennyson. Whatever else it means, it is the signature of a broken world. The successful metaphor would be the signature of repair and reach toward the ultimate order. This role of metaphor will be important in chapter 1, "Robert Frost and T. S. Eliot: Modernisms."

✦

In its search for order, modernism was in a sense *traditional,* a recurrent phenomenon, whether during periods of cultural confusion or simply to discern order amid multiple phenomena: the regularity of the heavenly bodies, the annual sequence of the seasons, the tides of the Aegean.

We see the search for such a principle early in the development of Western thought with thinkers known as the pre-Socratics. A man named Thales probably deserves to be called the first philosopher-scientist. Born in the small city of Miletus, he flourished in the early sixth century B.C. He is said to have predicted an eclipse of the sun later mentioned by Herodotus. He probably had some knowledge of planetary movements. In legend he is credited with discovering some of the theorems of Euclid (circa 300 B.C.) used in his *First Book* of geometry. According to remarks made by Aristotle in his magisterial *Metaphysics,* Thales concluded that the primary underlying substance of the cosmos is water.

Initially this sounds ludicrous. But the idea that there is a fundamental unifying factor or substance is momentous—central, indeed, to Socrates and Plato, not to mention modern quantum physics and the aspirations of its superconductor project, or speculations based upon the apparently limiting speed of light. Later Greek philosophy would call this underlying and unifying principle the Logos and engaged in profound debate about what it might be.

The Gospel of John opens, "In the beginning was the Word, and the Word was with God, and the Word was God. The same was in the beginning with God." The opening words "In the beginning" echo the opening of Genesis, and, in the third verse of Genesis we have, "God said, 'Let there be light.' " In the Hebrew Bible this was God's creating word. When John begins, "In the beginning was the Word," he used the Greek for *Word,* that is, *Logos.* Hellenism and Christianity converged.

In our own time Martin Heidegger, very much drawn to the pre-Socratics, wrote extensively on Parmenides and Heracleitus as he continued their search under special modern exigencies, discerning an underlying reality (Being, *Sein*) that is shared by all separate existences.

Anaximander, Anaximenes, Pythagoras, and Heracleitus contributed to the ancient discussion. Pythagoras, born on the island of Samos (circa 532 B.C.), established his own philosophical academy and believed mathematics to be the principle of order in the cosmos. Democritus (circa 460 B.C.) grew up in the small town of Abdera in Thrace. He thought the universal building blocks of the universe to be atoms, that they moved in a void according to universal principles and that they are not reducible to smaller entities. Centuries later the Roman poet Lucretius (96?–55 B.C.)

turned such atomic suppositions into a poem of epic length, *De rerum natura* (*On the Nature of Things*).

In Socrates and Plato the pre-Socratic issues of permanence and flux, truth and opinion, and the nature of the cosmos would receive a grand attempt at solution. In the *Symposium* Socrates sets forth the grounds of permanence, attributing this analysis to a priestess of Manitea named Diotima. This is probably a polite fiction since Socrates's exposition is so obviously superior to the contributions of the other participants in the symposium.

Briefly, the Knower and the Lover—they are the same thing—begins with the sensible world we all know and makes his way "upward by a right use of feeling." One could do this with any sensible object, person, or quality, such as justice, ethical behavior, or the state. At the distant end of such a process, accumulating these permanent essences or ideas, one might rise to the permanent idea of the whole, the Logos, the idea of all ideas, the reality for which the pre-Socratics had striven.

The difficulty of much modernist literature is part of its lasting strength. It makes a strenuous demand and engages the reader with a unique power, the act of reading requiring a special investment of mind and will as the reader participates in the creating of an order within the appearance of mystery or disorder.

> April is the cruelest month, breeding
> Lilacs out of the dead land, mixing
> Memory and desire, stirring
> Dull roots with spring rain.

But what does this vatic verse mean? It is a half metaphor, the rest of which must be supplied by the engaged reader. In technical language, we have the "tenor" (April, lilacs, spring rain), but without the "vehicle." When Shakespeare wrote, "All the world's a stage," the world is the tenor, the stage the vehicle. This is symbolist poetry, which requires the reader to work with the poem and in effect participate in creating the meaning of the poem. The gerunds here express movement but are being resisted: dead, dull roots. Something will be born: lilacs. But the birth is cruel. Does April suggest Easter? Was the rebirth at Easter cruel? The death before Easter certainly was cruel. The reader must engage those questions, and in doing so strive to create order out of the fragments of the poem that follow. As the voice of *The Waste Land* says: "These fragments I have shored against my ruins."

In his essay "Tradition and the Individual Talent" (1919), Eliot set forth the historical paradigm that is the background for his journey from Prufrock through *Four Quartets* (1943):

> Tradition . . . cannot be inherited, and if you want it you must obtain it by great labour. It involves, in the first place, the historical sense . . . involves a perception, not only of the pastness of the past, but of its presence; the historical sense compels a man to write not merely with his own generation in his bones, but with a feeling that the whole of the literature of Europe from Homer and within it the whole of the literature of his own country has a simultaneous existence and composes a simultaneous order. This historical sense, which is a sense of the timeless as well as of the temporal and of the timeless and temporal together, is what makes a writer traditional.

In 1919 Eliot looked forward to *The Waste Land* and back to the entire range of European literature. In particular, Eliot looked to the past for examples of a fragmented culture and responses to it, discerning four previous metaphysical moments: Dante in Florence during the thirteenth century; Donne and other Metaphysical poets in London during the seventeenth century; Laforgue in Paris during the nineteenth century; and presumably Eliot himself in London during the twentieth century.

Characteristic of Donne is the radical metaphor, putting highly disparate parts together to form a surprising unity. In his *First Anniversary: An Anatomy of the World* (1611), Donne had written his own *Waste Land,* the traditional order of his world shattered by science:

> And new Philosophy calls all in doubt,
> The Element of fire is quite put out;
> The Sun is lost, and th' earth, and no man's wit
> Can well direct him where to look for it.
> And freely men confess that this world's spent,
> When in the Planets and the Firmament
> They seek so many new: they see that this
> Is crumbled out again to his Atomies.
> 'Tis all in pieces, all coherence gone;
> All just supply, and all Relation:
> Prince, Subject, Father, Son, are things forgot,
> For every man alone thinks he hath got
> To be a Phoenix, and that there can be
> None of that kind of which he is, but he.

Copernicus's theory based on observation (1543) that the universe is heliocentric had become increasingly accepted. This removed the earth from centrality, as God surely would have given it, and for Donne subverted everything ("all"). The traditional order of the elements (fire, air, water, earth) was also being questioned. The social hierarchy had lost its natural validity with individualism emerging.

In Donne we get the radical metaphor, as if by force of imagination relation might be restored. For example, in "A Valediction: Forbidding Mourning," as he plans a trip abroad, he compares the intensity of the lovers' love to gold beaten thin, and also to compasses:

> Dull sublunary lovers' love
>   (Whose soul is sense) cannot admit
> Absence, because it doth remove
>   Those things which elemented it.
>
> But we by a love so much refined,
>   That ourselves know not what it is,
> Inter-assurèd of the mind,
>   Care less eyes, lips, and hands to miss.
>
> Our two souls therefore, which are one,
>   Though I must go, endure not yet
> A breach, but an expansion,
>   Like gold to aery thinness beat.
>
> If they be two, they are two so
>   As stiff twin compasses are two;
> Thy soul the fixed foot makes no show
>   To move, but doth, if th' other do.
>
> And though it in the centre sit,
>   Yet when the other far doth roam,
> It leans, and hearkens after it,
>   And grows erect as that comes home.
>
> Such wilt thou be to me, who must
>   Like th' other foot obliquely run;
> Thy firmness makes my circle just
>   And makes me end where I begun.

Those radical metaphors exhibit wit, but they also represent the rhetorical signature of imagination. The lovers (tenor) are pulled together with the radically different vehicles "gold to airey thinness beat" and "stiff twin compasses." Eliot's evening "spread out against the sky / Like a patient etherized upon a table" fails to bring tenor and vehicle together, reestablishing the relations within a severely broken world. As Lionel Trilling once remarked to me, "In every metaphor the Logos is implicit." He added, "even the lowly pun." Both of those rhetorical forms see similarity within difference.

Eliot began a long Dantean journey with "The Love Song of J. Alfred Prufrock" (1915), which was then incorporated into *Prufrock and Other Observations* (1917). The broken metaphor with which it begins represents a broken world that will not become whole again until the unity signified by the final line of "Little Gidding," the fourth and final *Quartet*. The long journey begins this way:

> Let us go then, you and I,
> When the evening is spread out against the sky
> Like a patient etherized upon a table.

The third line rejects the expansive first two lines, and *Like* is false.

Epigraphs are especially important here at the beginning. The epigraph to "The Love Song" comes from Dante's *Inferno*. We infer that Prufrock is damned, but that the Dantean journey is beginning. Apparently Eliot envisioned the course his journey would take. Indeed, it does take a long journey from the fractured metaphor with which "The Love Song of J. Alfred Prufrock" begins to the unity at the end of "Little Gidding": "And the fire and the rose are one."

At the end of "Little Gidding," the fire of purgation has become one with the rose of love. The difficulty of achieving such identity, the struggle required to see similarity in dissimilarity, reflects the power of the disorder against which the poem exerts its energies. (Joyce's *Ulysses* appeared in 1922, the same year as *The Waste Land,* and used Homer's *Odyssey* to structure the chaos of experience, the "mythical method," as Eliot called it.)

In his poems, Robert Frost conducted a long-running war against T. S. Eliot, pitting his own naturalism, an open naturalism in the mode of William James, against T. S. Eliot's visionary transcendentalism, the "still point," the moment "in-and-out-of-time" that Eliot called "incarnation." Robert Frost is not usually considered a modernist, but in early reviews both the poet Edward Thomas and Ezra Pound, the impresario of modernism, identified new elements in his verse that indeed identified him as such, as will be seen in chapter 1.

Though modernism appeared long before the First World War, first in France and later in England, it went mainstream after the war, as the nineteenth century had been blown away by the mass killings on the Somme and elsewhere. The modernism of Hemingway's *In Our Time* (1925), with its fragmentary structure reflecting the brokenness of the world and requiring the reader to find relations among them, resembles *The Waste Land* and was now popular reading, published by Boni and Liveright. With the help of Conrad and Eliot, F. Scott Fitzgerald's modernism was also mainstream. In *The Great Gatsby*, Jay Gatsby, a romantic idealist, collides with the brutal realism of Tom Buchanan, and at the end Gatsby lies dead in his swimming pool. Fitzgerald has put various elements together—Gatsby, Daisy and Tom Buchanan, Myrtle and George Wilson—and lets them interact, Gatsbyism strewing corpses along the north shore of Long Island. But finally, even though Gatsby himself is dead, the moon of Gatsby's romantic hope rises again over the "waste land" landfill called the valley of ashes, which is presided over by the empty spectacles of Dr. T. J. Eckleburg, a Deus absconditus. The reader might well think of Eliot's *Waste Land*. Indeed, after the 1922 *Waste Land*, no reader of *The Great Gatsby* (1925) could read the words *valley of ashes*, described as a "waste land," without thinking of Eliot's poem, the most influential poem written (mostly) in English during the twentieth century.

Surely Nick Carraway is right when he judges that Gatsby is "worth the whole damned bunch" of them because of his romantic idealism, even as Owl Eyes is right when he says of Gatsby "the poor son of a bitch." Though both judgments are right, Nick has the last word when, in his beautiful final prose elegy, he sees Gatsby, with his "capacity for wonder," as exemplifying the American, and continuous with those original Dutch sailors:

> And as the moon rose higher the inessential houses began to melt away until gradually I became aware of the old island here that flowered once for Dutch sailors' eyes—a fresh, green breast of the new world. Its vanished trees, the trees that had made way for Gatsby's house, had once pandered in whispers to the last and greatest of human dreams; for a transitory enchanted moment man must have held his breath in the presence of this continent, compelled

into an aesthetic contemplation he neither understood nor desired,
face to face for the last time in history with something commensu-
rate to his capacity for wonder.

A great many complex thoughts operate in this passage and in this novel.

Reflect, for example, on the verb *pandered* in this passage, and also on
that "fresh, green breast" along with such "flowers" as Daisy and Myrtle.
The thoughts may be contradictory but also true, and America may in
fact be the "green light" at the end of the Buchanan dock, America the
country of the future and aspiration. As we respond to this novel with
its contradictions, its honesty, we encounter the variousness, complexity,
and difficulty of actual life, to echo the phrase in Lionel Trilling's famous
preface to *The Liberal Imagination* (1950).

Literature worthy of the name does not merely communicate. The best
prose and poetry make things happen, constitute an awakening for the
receptive mind. In all times and places people have felt that variously
exigent circumstances discourage; the hurrying moment, the cataract of
time, has always and at all times swept us forward, interfering with the
fully lived life—yes, always the case, but anyone today can sense the special character, perhaps even the uniqueness, of our situation.

There is truth in what Susan Sontag wrote in *Against Interpretation:*
"All the conditions of modern life—its material plentitude, its sheer
crowdedness—conjoin to dull our sensory faculties. . . . We must learn to
see more, to *hear* more, to *feel* more."

As if in answer to Susan Sontag's cri de coeur, Marilynne Robinson's
Gilead appeared in 2004, a distinctively modernist novel, modernism
remaining relevant. *Gilead* slows the action down, enabling its first-
person narrator to absorb and reflect upon his experience. Set in the small
Iowa town of Gilead in the year 1957, this novel consists of a long letter
written by the local pastor, John Ames, to his seven-year-old son by his
second and much younger wife. The epistolary form is essential to the
central subject of this novel, the special perceptiveness of the Rev. John
Ames. Ames has angina and knows that he may soon die. Before reading
the book I noticed a remark in a review by the critic James Wood that
Gilead's prose reflects a mind "in which silence is itself a quality, and in
which the space around words may be full of noises." That observation
surely was enough to attract anyone's attention.

The Rev. John Ames's ability to respond to the moment amounts to
a kind of genius, surely sharpened by his awareness of his own mortality. Though he is a very learned man, there is no evidence here that he is
aware of Martin Heidegger, who discerned a depth of experience within

the chaos of ordinary consciousness. Yet Ames does experience what Martin Heidegger called Being, that is, the felt weight of *isness* as against a surrounding and sharply contrasting nothingness. Heidegger thought we needed the courage to face the anxiety and encounter the actuality of Being (*Sein*). He quoted Hölderlin: "Celebration is . . . attentiveness . . . is waiting, is a step over into the more wakeful glimpse of the wonder—the wonder that a world is existing around us at all, that there are beings rather than nothing." The Rev. John Ames sometimes has such perception in precisely Heidegger's sense:

> I was struck by the way the light felt that afternoon. I have paid a good deal of attention to light, but no one could begin to do it justice. There was the feeling of a weight of light—pressing the damp out of the grass and pressing the smell of sour old sap out of the boards on the porch floor and burdening even the trees a little as a late snow would do.

Heidegger's *Being and Time* appeared in 1927, and Heidegger's experience of the moment of vision, when the perception of Being occurs, is analogous to decisive moments experienced by contemporaries, such as T. S. Eliot's experience of the "still point," the moment in-and-out-of-time that he called "incarnation," the penetration of time by eternity; Carl Schmitt's "moment of decision"; Ernst Jünger's "sudden fright"; Paul Tillich's *kairos,* the moment of fate and decision when "eternity erupts into time"; and Kierkegaard's "moment," when God burst into his life and he felt summoned to risk the leap into faith. Finally here, in Thomas Mann's *Doctor Faustus,* the "moment" will come as a single note in a modernist musical composition, a note that points beyond time. Heidegger recognized the reality of the special moment, but he did not connect it with God or Christianity.

What follows here is an examination of important works of literature as they seek to explore the experience of living in a broken world, with thought and sometimes with examples of resolve, as in Hemingway, that possess permanent validity.

CHAPTER ONE

Robert Frost and T. S. Eliot: Modernisms

Literature is news that STAYS news.
—Ezra Pound, *ABC of Reading*

At first the disproportion between Robert Frost and T. S. Eliot seems immense. In relation to Eliot, Frost's reputation suffered from his popularity among readers of the middle range of discernment, a popularity he cultivated through his public persona. Eliot, first famous with *The Waste Land,* conceded nothing to readers of that middle range, but he was hailed as a champion of modernism and possessed enormous authority among the most discerning. But such differences in reputation are extraneous to the merits of the poetry itself. Together Frost and Eliot constitute polarities of energy that have been intrinsic to American culture; their success in expressing this struggle would not have been possible had they been other than powerful writers.

During the summer of 1912 Robert Frost took a big gamble. If he succeeded in gaining recognition, he would continue to strive as a poet. If he failed, he would quit. He had taught successfully in New Hampshire, published poetry in obscure journals, and now had some assets in the form of his Derry farm, purchased for him by his grandfather, as well as an annuity of $500 from that grandfather's estate. On August 23, 1912, he sold the farm and sailed from Boston with his wife, Elinor, and their young children to England. It would be recognition or defeat.

They rented a cottage in Beaconsfield. Frost spread out his poems on the floor and arranged them in a sequence reflecting the shifting moments of a young man's mind. Completely unknown in England, he submitted those poems over the transom to the publisher David Nutt in London. The manuscript was accepted and appeared as *A Boy's Will* on April 23, 1913. The American poet, who had been born in San Francisco, who had spent

his childhood there, but who was thought accurately to be a quintessen-
tially New England poet, first achieved recognition in London. A year later,
on May 14, Nutt published *North of Boston*, with the publisher Henry
Holt in Boston contracting for American rights and henceforth serving as
Frost's publisher. Meanwhile Frost circulated among the London literary
figures, including Ezra Pound, William Butler Yeats, and, most important
for Frost, Edward Thomas, a literary journalist known both for his accurate perceptions about literature and for being among the earliest readers
to understand the special qualities of Pound's poetry. In F. M. Ford's *English
Review* Thomas had considered Pound's *Personae* (1909), distinguishing it
from the melancholy and preciosity of the Edwardians and praising the
firsthand intensity of feeling realized in its verse: "He has . . . hardly any of
the superficial good qualities of modern versifiers. . . . [He is] full of personality and with such power to express it, that from the first to last lines
of most of his poems he holds us steadily in his own pure grave passionate
world." Thomas would be an excellent ambassador for Frost to the new
literary circles in London, in which Pound was a central figure.

In the three years that remained of Thomas's life, he and Frost became
intense literary and personal friends. Thomas, burdened with oppressive
self-consciousness, felt emboldened by Frost's determination and proceeded to realize *himself* as a poet, producing a remarkable number of
good poems, clearly influenced by Frost, during the few years before his
death at Arras in April 1917. In his study of this friendship, Matthew
Spencer titled his book *Elected Friends: Robert Frost and Edward Thomas
to One Another*, alluding to Goethe's *Elective Affinities*, with its allusion
to Calvin's theology of God's "predestined elect."[1] In English periodicals
useful to Frost's struggle for recognition, Thomas wrote three reviews of
North of Boston. In the *London Daily News* of July 22, 1914, Thomas
began, "This is one of the most revolutionary books of modern times, but
one of the quietest and least aggressive." This is felicitous. Frost was a
concealed modernist, unlike the theatrical and insurgent Pound. Though
a modernist, Frost never appeared in magazines with such titles as *Vortex*,
Blast, or *Broom*. In the *New Weekly* of August 8, 1914, Thomas again
reviewed *North of Boston* and also discussed *A Boy's Will*: "Mr. Frost has
in fact gone back, as Whitman and as Wordsworth went back, through
the paraphernalia of poetry into poetry once again." He reviewed *North
of Boston* for a third time in the *English Review* of August 1914: Frost
had "refused the 'glory of words,' which is the modern poet's embarrassment. . . . Only at the end of the best pieces, such as 'The Death of the
Hired Man,' 'Home Burial,' 'The Black Cottage,' and 'The Woodpile,' do
we realize that they are masterpieces of deep and mysterious tenderness."

In terms of furthering Frost's nascent career, two reviews by Ezra Pound—famous as an impresario of modernism and possessing an exceptionally acute sense of language—were especially welcome. His review of *A Boy's Will* appeared in the *New Freewoman* (London, September 1913) and concentrated on Frost's fresh verisimilitude. Through apt quotation Pound demonstrates, without analysis, the presence of new elements in his verse. Perhaps this omission reflected haste, since that same year in *Patria Mia* (an important work, written in 1913 but languishing in a publisher's files until 1950 when it was finally published), Pound defined some new, or recovered from the past, elements of style that would characterize Frost. A year later, writing in Harriet Monroe's influential *Poetry* (December 1914), he showed more attention to Frost's verse in his treatment of *North of Boston*.[2] Pound's reviews (later collected in his literary essays) were important for Frost as an indication of regard by the leader of the modernist movement. In 1915 Pound virtually forced Harriet Monroe to publish Eliot's "Love Song of J. Alfred Prufrock" in *Poetry*, though she did not understand the poem.

In *Patria Mia* Pound depicts the United States as barren of poetic culture and pointedly observes that the renaissance of the arts in Italy had been the work of a relatively small group of like-minded men, no doubt having himself in mind as the leader of such a cohort promoting a new renaissance with modernism as its unifying cause. In *Patria Mia* Pound also analyzes what he admires in the English language—and what the moment cried out for. This was the best analysis then, and perhaps now, of what Frost was accomplishing in his verse. Pound argues that modernism has "strengthened it [the English language] and given it fibre. And this is hardly more than a race conviction *that words scarcely become a man* [italics added]. . . . [The] man is the man ready for his deed, eager for it, eager for the glory of it, ready to pay the price. If a man has this quality and be meagre of speech one asks little beyond this." (Pound finds a quality such as this in Whitman, words held close to action: "Camerado, this is no book;/Who touches this touches a man.") Pound continues, "Here is a spirit, one might say, as hostile to the arts as was *the Anglo-Saxon objection to speaking at all* [italics added]. . . . The strength of both peoples [English and American] is just here; that one undertakes to keep quiet until there is something worth saying."[3] When Edward Thomas enlisted in the British army on July 19, 1915, Frost praised him as "a man of words and deeds, a man of his word, a man." There Frost would have been echoing *Patria Mia* had that essay been available to him. As Frost wrote to Thomas on November 6, 1916, "Talk is almost too cheap when all your friends are facing bullets. I don't believe I ought to enlist (since I am of course an American), but if I can't enlist, at least I refuse to talk sympathy beyond a certain point." Thomas had used the phrase "a language not to be betrayed" in his poem "I Never Saw That Land Before." Frost wrote a poem conveying this verbal reticence, "On Talk of Peace at This Time":

> France. France, I know not what is in my heart.
> But God forbid that I should be more brave
> As watcher from a quiet place apart
> Than you are who are fighting in an open grave. . . .
>
> Not mine to say you shall not think of peace,
> Not mine, not mine, I almost know your pain.

Thomas (December 31, 1916), now a second lieutenant, replied with perfect tact that the poem "expresses just those hesitations you or I would have at asking others to act as we think it is their cue to act. Well, I am soon going to know more about it." After this, Frost, valuing silence here, appropriately never published the poem.[4] Thomas was killed on April 9, 1917.

Writing from a wartime perspective, Frost and Thomas were nonetheless emphasizing what Pound had said about all serious writing: that every word must count, that writing must possess integrity, and that there are times when silence is the only form integrity can take. Pound had enjoined, "One undertakes to keep quiet until there is something worth saying." Frost also wrote a very fine poem, "Not to Keep," probably in the spring of 1916, not about Thomas but likely inspired by him, the entire poem working hard to charge the four plain words in its last line with great force. Here, a wounded soldier has come home to his wife to rest and recuperate. "And she could have him," says the letter from the front. His wife inquires, "What was it, dear?" The soldier answers,

>   "Enough,
> Yet not enough. A bullet through and through,
> High in the breast. Nothing but what good care
> And medicine and rest, and you a week,
> Can cure me of to go again." The same
> Grim giving to do over for them both.
> She dared no more than ask him with her eyes
> How was it with him for a second trial.

And with his eyes he asked her not to ask.
They had given him back to her, but not to keep.

Here words disappear into complete silence, and not only for "a man" but
for a woman as well. Only silence could speak under pressure from emotion so powerful. The poem works effectively for those last four words,
words indeed of wide human application. "Not to Keep" appeared in
the *Yale Review* (January 1917) and was reprinted in *New Hampshire*
(1923). That volume would be a central document in Frost's poetic battle against T. S. Eliot, whose *Waste Land* appeared both in England and
America in 1922 and now held aloft the banner of modernism.

Eliot, in his *Ezra Pound: His Metric and Poetry* (1917), had shown
through his close analysis of Pound's early verse how specific his high
estimate of his craftsmanship could be. Until the publication in 1971 of a
facsimile draft of *The Waste Land* typescript showing Pound's deletions
and corrections, we did not realize the extent of his role. Pound cut a fifty-
four-line passage of dialogue at the beginning, made other cuts, tightened
the poem overall—made its reader work harder between passages—and
in total effect intensified its modernism. Pound was more than an editor
here—but not quite a coauthor. When we become aware of Pound's large
role in shaping *The Waste Land,* we are not surprised that Eliot dedicated
it "For Ezra Pound *il miglior fabbro* [the better craftsman]." This repeated
the compliment Dante bestows upon Arnaut Daniel in *Purgatorio* (canto
xxvi), judging him superior to all his rival Provençal poets. In later cor-
respondence, Eliot characterized the original *Waste Land* as "a sprawling,
chaotic poem," which Pound "reduced to almost half its size."[5]

The Waste Land begins with half a metaphor:

April is the cruelest month, breeding
Lilacs out of the dead land, mixing
Memory and desire, stirring
Dull roots with spring rain.

Arresting, especially the rhyming gerunds trying to move the resisting
nouns, but where is the rest of the metaphor? What does it all mean?
Those are the wrong questions. The meaning of these four lines, con-
veyed by the language, the poem's distinctive idiom, partly issues from
its voice—or voices. *The Waste Land* begins with a mysterious voice,
that of a shaman, perhaps, or a witch doctor, with the noise of drums
beating in the jungle. James M. Cox has made a useful distinction in
declaring that Eliot's poetry has "the sense of sound" while Frost's has the

"sound of sense." Frost himself used the latter phrase to characterize his poetry.

The Waste Land made an immediate impact, receiving forty-six reviews in the United States and England, about equally divided between approval and condemnation. Alert readers sensed its power even as they were bewildered. In November 1922 the poet John Peale Bishop wrote to his friend Edmund Wilson, "I have read *The Waste Land* about five times a day since the copy of the *Criterion* came into my hands. It is immense, magnificent, terrible." Burton Rascoe called it "perhaps the finest poem of this generation," a poem of "sheer verbal loveliness, enough ecstasy, enough psychological verisimilitude, and enough even of a readily understandable etching of modern life, to justify Mr. Eliot in his idiosyncrasies."[6] William Carlos Williams felt that *The Waste Land* had blown away what he was trying to do in verse, recalling in his *Autobiography* that it "wiped out our world as if an atom bomb had been dropped upon it and our brave sallies into the unknown were turned to dust. . . . I felt at once that it had set me back twenty years." So commanding a presence did the poem soon become that if a reader dismissed it as unintelligible, such a reader committed cultural suicide and disappeared from serious discussion of poetry.

Mystery is integral to one reach of Eliot's meaning. Against Eliot's powerful and immensely influential *Waste Land*, Frost saw that he had to defend a poetic clearing in which his own poetry and its sound of sense could live, his own brand of modernism, quieter and less aggressive certainly than the spectacular *Waste Land*. The method of Frost's poetry differed widely from Eliot's. Fundamentally skeptical, Frost was wary of metaphor and needed to be persuaded of identities between disparate things; he used lyrics to test experience when he ventured a metaphor, testing even, or especially, contradictory experience. Metaphor had to be earned against the pressure of skepticism. Eliot placed metaphor at the center of his poetic world and arranged the entire sequence of his poems along the line of *The Divine Comedy*, the great traditional drama of damnation and salvation. His use of Dante was an example of the "mythic method" that Joyce, Pound, Yeats, Stravinsky, Picasso, and even Freud undertook. *The Waste Land* refers to myth and legend, even Sanskrit, as echoes of a vanished mind—of which the modern mind is a shrunken continuation. Frost hinted at myth sometimes but drew back when skepticism's breath touched the poem.

The cacophony of voices in *The Waste Land*, written in an extraordinary variety of rhythms, dramatizes the tormenting loudness and dissonance that direct the reader toward the longed-for divine silence.

Eliot arrived in London in September 1914 to the confusion of sounds in the imperial metropolis and was terribly dismayed. This letter to his aunt may prefigure *The Waste Land:*

> The noise hereabouts is like hell turned upside down. Hot weather, all windows open, many babies, pianos, street piano accordions, singers, hummers, whistlers. Every house has a gong: they all go off at seven o'clock, and other hours. Ten o'clock in the evening, quiet for a few minutes, then a couple of men with late editions burst into the street, roaring: GREAT GERMAN DISASTER! Everybody rushes to windows and doors, in every costume from evening clothes to pajamas; violent talking—English, American, French, Flemish, Russian, Spanish, Japanese; the papers are all sold in five minutes; then we settle down for another hour till the next extra appears: LIST OF ENGLISH DEAD AND WOUNDED. Meanwhile, a dreadful old woman, her skirt trailing on the street, sings "the Rosary" in front, and secures several pennies from windows and the housemaid resumes her conversation at the area gate.

Eliot adds that the noise becomes "attached to the city": "I find it quite possible to work in this atmosphere. The noises of a city so large as London don't distract one much; they become attached to the city and depersonalise themselves." In *The Waste Land* we again hear the voices and cacophonous sounds as they become the Unreal City.

Frost's voice is very far from that of shaman or witch doctor: instead it is the voice of rural New England, albeit a highly educated voice, skeptical, individualistic, testing all claims against a resistant, even unyielding actuality. Myth may appear in this rocky soil but hesitantly, against the strength of fact. The distinctive voice Frost evolved used an iambic meter modified by the rhythms of colloquial speech distributed in natural word order. This produced lines close to prose but nudged into verse by the latent iambics. As Frost put it, he sought to "get cadences by . . . breaking the sounds of sense with all their irregularity of accent across the regular beat of the meter." Here we have one aspect of Frost's modernism, his use of the vernacular in this way, though with slang filtered out. He was alert to tonalities, simple words such as *yes* or *no* through tone meaning different things. He also sought to speak with indirection in a poem, telling the truth "slantwise," as he put it, no doubt to make the poem represent for the reader the process of seeking the meaning, or, to put it another way, making the reader work for the truth. In this kind of difficulty he demanded effort of his readers, as Eliot did, the required effort not so easily grasped at first. Frost, as much as Pound or Eliot, considered his procedures revolutionary: to his friend Hyde Cox, Frost writes from England that "the book [*North of Boston*] is epoch-making. I don't ask anyone to say so. All I ask now is to be allowed to live."[7]

Unwilling to be easily or carelessly known, Frost practiced several kinds of elusiveness and difficulty, explaining in "Directive," from *Steeple Bush* (1947), that a journey is necessary "so the wrong ones can't find it,/ So can't get saved, as Saint Mark says they mustn't." In Mark 4:11–12 Jesus says that he speaks in parables so that those will understand who should understand, not outsiders, and so gain the secret of "the kingdom of God." The kingdom from which Frost's "wrong ones" are excluded is the right kind of poetry—that is, Frost's. Illustrating this is one of Frost's most famous and celebrated poems (known but not known), "The Road Not Taken," from *Mountain Interval* (1916)—and, in view of its fame, a poem that excludes an enormous number of people because they do not pay attention and hear only one line, "I took the one less traveled by."

One evening, three or four years before Frost died in 1963, I found myself in an audience of about three hundred "wrong ones" in New York's Town Hall. The white-haired old national legend was in fine energetic form, reciting his poems and commenting on them, full of pithy remarks about events of the day and a wide range of other matters, clearly delighted to perform as his invented "Robert Frost." Amid the more famous poems I remember his reciting the distich "Forgive O Lord, my little jokes on Thee,/ And then I'll forgive Thy great big one on me." Frost's age made his mortality dramatic. For his final poem he recited "The Road Not Taken" and was clearly pleased with the cascade of applause at the end. Or was he pleased about springing his trap on this audience? Remember that title: "The Road Not Taken." Not "The Road Less Traveled By." Now we will be more wary than that crowd in Town Hall. The poem begins:

> Two roads diverged in a yellow wood,
> And sorry I could not travel both
> And be one traveler, long I stood
> And looked down one as far as I could
> To where it bent in the undergrowth;

The tone is jaunty, but he must choose one: he cannot take both. That necessity introduces a touch of seriousness, the sacrifice of one possibility, the act of choice perhaps hastened by the (autumnal) yellow wood. He seems not to know his way at that moment of choosing. We sense some sadness in the fourth line and even more as the forsaken road disappears, as if forever. The jaunty note of line 3 ("and be one traveler") gives way to something more somber. Now comes the pivotal second stanza.

> Then took the other, as just as fair,
> And having perhaps the better claim,
> Because it was grassy and wanted wear;
> Though as for that the passing there
> Had worn them really about the same,

In line 3, the traveler puts forward the possibility that one road "wanted wear"—that is, it was "less traveled" than the other. Then the pivot intrudes with "Though" and is confirmed by "really." They are "really about the same." Neither road was "less traveled." That evident truth now is reaffirmed by stanza 3:

> And both that morning equally lay
> In leaves no step had trodden black.
> Oh, I kept the first for another day!
> Yet knowing how way leads on to way,
> I doubted if I should ever come back.

There we have the subject of this poem: choice. Genuine choice necessarily occurs when you choose between two essentially equal things. Were they unequal, there would be no choice, since you would choose the better one on whatever basis you made that judgment. Being offered either five dollars or ten dollars would not be a genuine choice. Genuine choice has a tragic quality, the canceling out of the good option in favor of one equally good. The title of the poem, "The Road Not Taken," identifies the tragic hero of this drama, a small tragedy—but maybe not so small in view of the excluding choices we make in life without being able to see the consequences. This poem is a parable; in life there may be major tragic choices, the lost option eventually seen as a refused great good.

But now in the final stanza strange things happen, seemingly inexplicable in view of what has gone before:

> I shall be telling this with a sigh
> Somewhere ages and ages hence:
> Two roads diverged in a wood, and I—

I took the one less traveled by,
And that has made all the difference.

In that final stanza Frost springs his trap. The last three lines, a bogus story he will be telling *with a sigh* (that should give the trap away) somewhere ages and ages hence (such as here tonight in Town Hall), amounts to a self-serving fabrication, a triumph and not a tragedy. The egotistical repetition of "I" in lines 3 and 4, with line 3 given an extra accented syllable, should warn the reader—and should have warned that Town Hall audience, if it had paid attention to the poem. The final stanza even foresees how the story will be embellished by that sigh, a rhetorical sigh. Frost knew that night what was coming: he had been in this situation before.

Even as the audience began to cheer and as the cheers swelled to a roar, Frost stood there on the stage with his arms extended over his head like a heavyweight champion. Which indeed he was. He stood there, arms in the air, as the cheering went on and even rebel yells rose in shrieks. He had sprung the trap. These people were not poetry readers. They enjoyed celebrity. They paid no attention to words. To them Frost was a conventional hero because he had chosen an individual and risky path. Not in that parable, though. We are right back in Mark 4:11–12. For those "who stand without . . . they must watch and watch, yet never see, and must listen and listen, yet never understand, nor ever turn back, and have their sins forgiven them." The kingdom of heaven, Frost's poetry, is not for them.

Why did Frost so often trick his reader? Because he wanted his reader to pay the closest possible attention to poems. His verse had the clarity of his classical masters, notably Catullus, and the chill of reason (or of "frost"). An "educational" movie exists about Frost. Its title?—*The Road Less Traveled By.*

Probably Frost sprang his biggest trap before the largest audience a poet has ever had when he recited a poem at Kennedy's inauguration in 1961. He had written a poem for the occasion, about how the New Frontier would be a second "Augustan age" of "poetry and power." But, as he stood at the podium, the sun was too bright for him to see well, and wind blew his papers, so he recited from memory "The Gift Outright" from his volume *A Witness Tree* (1942). There is a great deal of beauty in Frost's poetry, but he wins this against a substratum of an unyielding realism, which is expressed in this poem on the history of Americans who are no longer the colonial settlers of Massachusetts and Virginia; they have earned the land by rendering a gift outright, the gift of themselves . . . by fighting, killing, and dying for the land.

> Such as we were we gave ourselves outright
> (The deed of gift was many deeds of war)
> To the land vaguely realizing westward,
> But still unstoried, artless, unenhanced,
> Such as she was, such as she would become.

The characterization of the land as a woman establishes the idea of the gift as a wedding gift—a fruitful yet not perfect marriage. The chill of realism enters strongly in the words "Such as she was." The pioneers and the cavalry were not perfect, nor are their descendants—"such as she would become," the wars of conquest haphazardly moving west. Still, the land was made real, realized through stories and art, and civilized, made into real estate. The West was won by fighting for it and it became our story (enhanced), such as it is.

How many listening at that inauguration of the New Frontier detected a touch of irony? How many present there or viewing from their living rooms on that festive day really heard Frost's poem? Who felt the chill of Frost beneath the January cold of that moment? Did the ladies and gentlemen of the press and television have any inkling? Probably they thought this was another safely patriotic poem. It was, indeed, about the "winning of the West," as Theodore Roosevelt called his multivolume narrative, and in Frost's poem those many deeds of war referred to a land soaked in the blood of many Indians and some soldiers and settlers. In the late seventeenth century in King Philip's War in central Massachusetts, more colonists were killed per capita than in any future American war; the surviving Indians were put on a small rocky island in Boston Harbor to freeze or starve. The final blood of the Indians in Frost's poem "The Vanishing Red" dyes a millstream red after the last Indian in Acton, a town near Boston, has been thrown down among the grinding stone mill wheels. "He is said to have been the last Red Man / In Acton." "Poking about the mill," John, the last Indian, makes a "guttural," savage sound the miller finds disgusting, perhaps an insult to his mill machinery. A narrator describes John's end:

> He took him down below a cramping rafter,
> And showed him, through a manhole in the floor,
> The water in desperate straits like frantic fish,
> Salmon and sturgeon, lashing with their tails.

Then he shut down the trap door with a ring in it
That jangled even above the general noise . . .
Oh, yes, he showed John the wheel pit all right.

We need not conclude that this local narrator telling the story is Frost, but the poem belongs to Frost—such as we were, such as we would become. Frost chooses to represent that history in this poem. We do not know to what extent Frost endorses the judgment of the narrator about this aspect of American history: "You'd have to have been there and lived it./Then you wouldn't have looked on it as just a matter/Of who began it between the two races." At a guess, Frost does endorse it, sees the Indian wars as a conflict of civilization—such as we were, such as we would become—and savagery. This agrees with Jefferson's opinion in one of the allegations against George III in the Declaration of Independence: "You'd have to have been there and lived it." Frost was not teaching Native American studies.

Frost's appearance at the Kennedy inauguration and his recitation of "The Gift Outright" were widely held to be a cultural triumph for the New Frontier, a slogan that acquires a certain irony in the context of "The Gift Outright." Did anyone around Kennedy know what they were getting, especially with "The Gift Outright"? In 1962 the Kennedy administration sent Frost to the Soviet Union, where he was a cultural success and talked with Khrushchev as if they were both heads of state. Frost also had a conversation with the great Russian poet Anna Akhmatova, who considered herself to be the embodiment of Russia. As possessors and guardians of their languages, they could stake that claim.

A settler himself—an American poet using English—Frost occasionally articulated his own declaration of independence, taking on European master spirits. After 1922 and *The Waste Land* this warfare reached out to include T. S. Eliot, who, after all, had become an Englishman by then— a masquerade to a considerable extent. Eliot does belong to American rather than British poetry, though he was a traditionalist and a Catholic of the Anglican branch, while Frost was an American individualist, learning from his own experience, and to the extent that he was religious easily identified as a Protestant. In Frost's poetry, metaphor has to test itself against the skepticism of prose; while in Eliot's poetry, as at the start of "Prufrock," we begin with another broken metaphor which is finally transformed through intellect and spiritual pilgrimage into an identity, as in the last line of "Little Gidding": "the fire and the rose are one." That line could not live in the skepticism of "the sound of sense." The American and the quasi Englishman were at terminal odds.

In "Desert Places," from *A Further Range* (1936), Frost counters the European Pascal, who had written in his *Pensées:* "The eternal silence of these infinite spaces frightens me." Frost replies: "I have it in me so much nearer home / To scare myself with my own desert places." Frost substitutes the dismissive "scare" for the more glamorous and European "frightens." Frost is not Kafka, Nietzsche, Pascal, and, deliberately, not Eliot.

Immediately after *The Waste Land* was published in 1922, Frost made a full-scale attack on Eliot's poem in *New Hampshire*. There, the title poem, written in mid-June of the same year, was pressed into service as part of a volume constructed to attack Eliot's poem. At 414 lines in length, "New Hampshire" approximately matches *The Waste Land* at 433. Against Eliot's poetic territory of a desert, Frost's territory is "New Hampshire," an imaginative creation like Wordsworth's Lake Country and Faulkner's Yoknapatawpha County. In *New Hampshire* the burden of the attack comes not with the title poem but with a display of very strong poems after it under the headings "Notes" and then "Grace Notes." Frost's "New Hampshire" is fertile, not sterile like Eliot's desert, which gives rise only to pseudoacademic footnotes.

The voice in "New Hampshire," a poem in the Horatian manner, is that of Frost's stage persona, a rural sage who exalts his state with humorous comparisons to other states but repeatedly undercuts them and in so doing peeks out from behind the persona. He does this also with abundant allusions to Emerson, Marlowe's *Faustus,* Plato, Darwin, and, at the end of the poem, he demolishes the native persona altogether:

> I choose to be a plain New Hampshire farmer
> With an income in cash of, say a thousand
> (From say, a publisher in New York City).
> It's restful to arrive at a decision,
> And restful just to think about New Hampshire.
> At present I am living in Vermont.

When he wrote that poem, Frost was living on his farm in South Shaftsbury, Vermont, and claimed to have written both this poem and the remarkable "Stopping by Woods on a Snowy Evening" in a single night of concentrated composition. In light of that withdrawal of seriousness at the end of "New Hampshire," and the general joshing tone of the whole, this title poem amounts to a pseudoantagonist of the powerful *Waste Land,* with the genuine riposte coming in the flow of lyrics in "Notes" and "Grace Notes."

In the successive editions of Frost's collected poems, the designations "Notes" and "Grace Notes" are omitted from the text, thus losing much of the meaning of the original Holt edition (in addition, the handsome woodcuts in this original volume are well worth inspection). Among the many fine poems in "Notes" and "Grace Notes" we find the famous "Stopping by Woods on a Snowy Evening"—its simplicity, pictorial qualities, and rhythms making it a part of one's memory after only a few readings. Its subject, far from simple, is the Renaissance argument about which is superior, the contemplative or the active life. Its first stanza sets the scene: a man driving a sleigh at night, and, stopping to gaze at some woods nearby, is anxious about being seen by the owner of the woods:

> Whose woods these are I think I know.
> His house is in the village though;
> He will not see me stopping here
> To watch his woods fill up with snow.

The enjambment of lines 3 and 4 expresses the man's relief that he probably will not be seen by the owner. The next stanza establishes an equivalence between the owner and the horse in their incomprehension:

> My little horse must think it queer
> To stop without a farmhouse near
> Between the woods and frozen lake
> The darkest evening of the year.

The horse, as the owner would be were he present, fails to understand (this equivalence hardly a compliment to the owner). It may or may not be important that this is the longest night of the year, and also Saint Lucy's Day, when darkness begins to turn toward light and Christmas is near at hand. If that connection is valid, then the enlightenment consists of the driver's understanding of his experience here, which now follows. The horse signals impatience, perhaps for barn and hay:

> He gives his harness bells a shake
> To ask if there is some mistake.
> The only other sound's the sweep
> Of easy wind and downy flake.

The sounds of the harness bells emphasize the quiet of the surrounding scene, and the second couplet begins the man's aesthetic experience, which intensifies:

> The woods are lovely, dark and deep.
> But I have promises to keep,
> And miles to go before I sleep,
> And miles to go before I sleep.

The full stop after "deep" signals the coming reversal at "But," as the man responds to the demands of practical duty. The sequence "lovely, dark and deep" reflects the movement of the man's mind toward and into the woods.

Outrageously, gratuitously, this line has been tampered with in successive Holt editions of the *Collected Poems*. The editor, Edward Connery Lathem, has added a second comma to that first line, which changes its meaning. The line now reads: "The woods are lovely, dark, and deep." That added comma renders the adjective "lovely" a third quality parallel with "dark" and "deep," whereas Frost's punctuation made the loveliness the *result* of the subsequent two qualities: "dark" and "deep." That is a huge difference. Frost's original line expresses the man's series of perceptions as he contemplates the woods and is drawn further into what constitutes the loveliness. Lathem has spackled commas through the poems, often distorting Frost's meaning; and the careful reader must make the necessary corrections to a corrupted edition.[8]

The repetition in the final two lines of this lyric registers the man's awareness of practical duties. Unlike the owner and the horse, he appreciates the valid demands of both the *vita contemplativa* (contemplative life) and the *vita activa* (active life), and in that is completely human. Just in what tone the last two lines should be read—peremptory, weary and reluctant, or stoically determined—is up to the reader and is part of the drama in which the reader is invited to participate. It is here, in this lyric and in the forty-three others in "Notes" and "Grace Notes" that Frost makes his effective challenge to *The Waste Land*.

In his famous "Birches" (*Mountain Interval,* 1916), Frost's antagonist is one of the greatest poets in the European tradition, Dante. "Birches" can be read as Frost's defense of his own poetic method against Dante, and also, read retrospectively, against the Dantista Eliot. Here Frost first backs away from metaphor, an especially extravagant one, and then earns his own homely and American metaphor with a boy bending a birch tree by swinging on it. Early in the poem he contemplates the effect of the sun on the ice that bends birch trees down (lines 10–20), coming to the conclusion of this sequence with, "Like girls on hands and knees that throw their hair / Before them over their heads to dry in the sun." But he has gone too far there, swinging too high, and he pulls back:

> But I was going to say when Truth broke in
> With all her matter-of-fact about the ice-storm
> I should prefer to have some boy bend them
> As he went out and in to fetch the cows—

"But" and "truth" fight against that metaphor. From this point until the end of the poem, Frost earns his own metaphor with the boy bending the birch tree *toward* heaven but then back to earth; and in this he defines his own poetry against Dante's one-hundred-canto metaphor that ends in heaven and stays there with "the Love that moves the sun and the other stars."

> It's when I'm weary of considerations,
> And life is too much like a pathless wood
> Where your face burns and tickles with the cobwebs
> Broken across it, and one eye is weeping
> From a twig's having lashed across it open.

Frost knows that wood; the hypermetric third line signals that, followed by specific details of experience. His "wood" is more felt than Dante's famous dark wood in canto 1. But then Frost's speaker rejects Dante's heaven for the known earth:

> I'd like to get away from earth awhile
> And then come back to it and begin over.
> May no fate willfully misunderstand me
> And half grant what I wish and snatch me away
> Not to return. . . .

At that point the movement of the verse in the third and fourth lines swings as far as it will go, extending its movement with the enjambment between the fourth and then the fifth lines, and then reverses: "Earth's the right place for love: / I don't know where it's likely to go better." The circumscribed "I don't know" here is limiting and definitive. Frost is not the village atheist. He does not *know* that heavenly love is not in fact better.

But he does know earth, and he chooses it. Frost will not go a millimeter beyond what he knows. From that generalization the speaker returns to the literal birch tree:

> I'd like to go by climbing a birch tree,
> And climb black branches up a snow-white trunk
> *Toward* heaven, till the tree could bear no more,
> But dipped its top and set me down again.

He has made his choice from what he knows. Perhaps Frost helped his reader a bit too much by italicizing the word *toward;* though, as well as being a major poem, this is a polemic. Its controlling skepticism embraces what it says about earth being the right place for love: "I don't know where it's likely to go better." The poet chooses experience over hope and possibility, and in that way compares with William James's philosophy of experience, which does not deny the metaphysical possibility but concentrates on experience. Frost, early in his life, had read *The Will to Believe* and had taught in New Hampshire schools James's *Pragmatism* and his *Psychology*—known by Harvard students in the abbreviated version (used also by Frost) as "the jimmy." He found James a kindred spirit in his empiricism and philosophical openness.

As a lyric poet, catching experience in varied moments, Frost may see things contradictorily, depending on moment and mood. He does not drive, as do Eliot and Dante, toward a reckoning, a salvation. For this inconsistency the rationalist critic Yvor Winters condemned him as a "spiritual drifter." Frost's empiricism, like that of James, does not exclude possibilities beyond the world defined by the five senses, as in perhaps "Fragmentary Blue" or "For Once, Then, Something," or in the mysterious "After Apple-Picking":

> My long two-pointed ladder's sticking through a tree
> Toward heaven still,
> And there's a barrel that I didn't fill
> Beside it . . .

Much or little can be made of those first few lines: the mysterious quality of the rest of the poem suggests much, but Frost lets you do it on your own. If you wish to say with Yvor Winters that this is irresponsible on Frost's part, Frost could reply that he has gone as far as he honestly can go, and that life is like that. In "For Once, Then, Something," a man

kneels beside a well, gazing at the surface of the water below. First he sees
a reflection of himself:

> . . . the water
> Gives me back in a shining surface picture
> Me myself in the summer heaven godlike
> Looking out of a wreath of fern and cloud puffs.

In this parable man seems to be divinized, as is reinforced by the egotism
of "Me myself." In that moment, what the man sees is reality. But there
is more:

> *Once*, when trying with chin against a well-curb,
> I discerned, as I thought, beyond the picture,
> Through the picture, a something white, uncertain,
> Something more of the depths—and then I lost it.

The italicized word *Once* calls attention to the comical element here.
This man, apparently often, might be spotted looking down into wells in
a kneeling position. As if in prayer? This absurd behavior suggests that
he is driven by more than idle curiosity. As ripples in the surface of the
water erase his vision of "something," he asks, "What was that white-
ness? / Truth? A pebble of quartz? / For once, then, something." The poem
seems to take that "something" far more seriously than merely a piece of
quartz. But still it remains only something.

The last major engagement Frost undertook with Eliot came in "Directive." By 1947 Frost had *Four Quartets* in hand; "Little Gidding" had
appeared in 1942, completing Eliot's journey from "Prufrock" in 1915.
The entire oeuvre could be seen as a journey, or a quest for the Holy Grail
adumbrated in *The Waste Land*. In the many Grail legends this was the
cup Jesus drank from at the Last Supper. It was taken to Britain by Joseph
of Arimathea, where, being lost, it was sought by many knights. The
Grail, if found, would purify their lands and render them fertile again.
The seekers underwent ordeals that purified them, but only Galahad, of
perfect purity, saw the Grail and then died. Frost's "Directive" possesses
all the elements of a quest, but in homely New England form, where the
Grail is found at the end and turns out to be a broken child's cup. Full
of allusions, the poem echoes Wordsworth's sonnet "The World Is Too
Much With Us: Late and Soon" in Frost's "this now too much for us," as
well as *Walden*'s old and ruined houses simplifying the past. The past was

not simple, of course, but in "Directive" we are to be refreshed by a past "made simple." The poem begins with an invitation by a mysterious guide to travel upward along a mountain path carved by glaciers, grooved (and purified?) by ice and iron wagon wheels, and having "a certain coolness" as of geological time. The traveler / quester is invited to go "Back out of all this now too much for us, / Back in a time made simple by the loss / Of detail, burned, dissolved, and broken off / Like graveyard marble sculpture in the weather." The past only seems simple. Its imagined simplicity might be a relief to the troubled man of the present, as in pastoral poetry. Pursuing this journey with the guide, the quester undergoes "ordeals," as in the Grail legends: he senses ghostly presences; there is the menacing mention of "Panther Mountain," a name invented for this poem for its intimation of peril; and then encounters the old "firkins" (antique barrels), which seem to be mysteriously looking at the journeying man. The goal now is a lost village, out of the declining northern New England of Frost's poetic world. "There is a house that is no more a house / Upon a farm that is no more a farm / And in a town that is no more a town." We have seen these things before in Frost's poetry, facts of his New Hampshire with its subsistence farmers, artisans, lost sheep, abandoned dairy industries, and empty and crumbling houses—all of this long before the present gentrification. The guide, who must be Frost, "only has at heart your getting lost"— that is, lost from the present and so able to recover a better self, as in Luke 9:24: "For whosoever will save his life shall lose it; but whosoever will lose his life for my sake, the same shall save it." That is, gain the holiness taught in the Sermon on the Mount and the parables. The quest here leads through haunting trials, as in the Grail legends, climbing the mountain and ending "where two village cultures faded / Into each other. Both of them are lost. / And if you're lost enough to find yourself / By now, pull in your ladder road behind you." Among the shards of the dead village there remain a few pitiful things:

> First there's the children's house of make believe,
> Some shattered dishes underneath a pine,
> The playthings in the playhouse of the children.
> Weep for what little things could make them glad.
> Then for the house that is no more a house,
> But only a belilaced cellar hole,
> Now slowly closing like a dent in dough.

Left now for the traveler after this ordeal, a confrontation with time and mortality, must be the Grail itself:

Your destination and your destiny's
A brook that was the water of the house,
Cold as a spring as yet so near its source,
Too lofty and original to rage.
(We know the valley streams that when aroused
Will leave their tatters hung on barb and thorn.)

The reader by now must have an inkling of what those contrasting streams represent. The guide, however, a Virgil to the quester's pilgrim Dante, proffers a drink from the Grail:

I have kept hidden in the instep arch
Of an old cedar at the waterside
A broken drinking goblet like the Grail
Under a spell so the wrong ones can't find it,
So can't get saved, as Saint Mark says they mustn't.
(I stole the goblet from the children's playhouse.)
Here are your waters and your watering place.
Drink and be whole again beyond confusion.

Frost has said more than once that poetry is a "momentary stay against confusion," meaning that an achieved poem creates a permanent shape amid unruly and even chaotic experience. Those last lines promise much more—"whole again beyond confusion."

A plausible interpreter might notice that it is Frost's poem "Directive," directing as it does toward the rest of his poems about this New England, that has led us to this goal, "Cold [Frost] as a spring yet [still] so near its source." Near, one supposes, the sources of the English language. What is this but Frost's own language, classical in its purity and lucidity, but cold in its realism. While the individual form of a poem is a stay against confusion, the entire canon, the whole draught as it were, rewards the pilgrim to it with a condition "whole again beyond confusion." And Frost, "too lofty and original to rage" ("lofty," as in near its origin), is unlike those valley streams below, raging and leaving detritus. With those valley streams, it might be thought, Frost points toward the poet of *The Waste Land,* who, like Arnold, "took dejectedly / His seat upon the intellectual throne" ("New Hampshire").

Silence as a powerful force is present in all of Eliot's poetry—even amid the cacophonous voices of *The Waste Land,* it is present through its painful absence. The power of silence comes from the fact that it is the gateway to something beyond the empirical world. That Frost was aware of this quality may be suggested by "For Once, Then, Something." In Eliot that sense of something radically different from the ordinary world of the senses is much more powerfully present and rooted in experiences which Eliot describes, and of which we cannot doubt the authenticity. James had studied such experiences, without discounting the possibility that they are cognitive, in *The Varieties of Religious Experience.* In *The Use of Poetry and the Use of Criticism* (1933), Eliot remembers that as a child of ten, while exploring the beach at Cape Ann, he once peered into a rock pool and saw there a sea anemone for the first time. This was, he remembers, "not so simple, for an exceptional child, as it looks." Lyndall Gordon comments in *T. S. Eliot: An Imperfect Life* that "his imagination fastened, too, on the still pool and the light-filled water that recurred in his poetry as a tantalizing memory of unspeakable bliss."

In his essay on Dante (1929), Eliot discusses *La vita nuova* and Dante's transforming encounter at age nine with the child Beatrice in the streets of Florence. Her beauty is a vision for the child Dante of the necessarily divine possibility in the world. Robert Hollander argues that Dante's Beatrice is Christ who rebukes man's sins, not Mary the intercessor. Hollander argues that Dante used her in this way as a radical protest against the church of his time for not teaching or obeying Christ. Eliot's engagement with Dante's childhood vision of Beatrice is clearly personal. He says at the end of his discussion of *La vita nuova* that he has consulted with a psychologist about Dante's experience and wonders whether it might have happened earlier than age nine. Showing some expert knowledge, he thinks such experiences usually occur a few years earlier. Eliot alarmingly gives us an offhand observation that the "love of man and woman (or for that matter man and man) is only explained and made reasonable by the higher love, or else is simply the coupling of animals." This astonishing notion, that the body is not enjoyable for its own sake, probably was part of the tangle of emotions that were involved with his disastrous first marriage to Vivienne Haigh-Wood, which brought him to nervous collapse, an element of the emotions informing *The Waste Land.*

Another of Eliot's numinous experiences occurred at the time of his Harvard commencement in June 1910. Walking in the busy streets of Boston, he felt that he had suddenly shed all that was going on around him and experienced an enormous—momentarily terrifying, he writes—sense of peace, a sensation he described in a manuscript poem titled "Silence":

This is the ultimate hour
When life is justified.
The seas of experience
That were so broad and deep,
So immediate and steep,
Are suddenly still.
You may say what you will
At such peace I am terrified.
There is nothing else beside. [italics added]

This is the very weak verse of a college senior, but its italicized lines gain in importance retrospectively. Much at Harvard provided Eliot with a structure within which to focus on such an experience and to evaluate it as cognitive regarding the nature of actuality. Dante was enjoying a vogue at Harvard: Santayana, with whom Eliot took a course in the philosophy of history, was discussing Dante as one of his three philosophical poets; and Longfellow, Harvard professor of poetry, had ably translated *The Divine Comedy.* While an undergraduate, Eliot always carried with him a copy of the *Commedia* in the original Italian. He studied Sanskrit (then thought to be the origin of the Indo-European languages), and he also immersed himself in the Christian saints and mystics, making extensive notes on Evelyn Underhill's *Mysticism.* Concentrating academically in philosophy and at the same time destined for the Harvard philosophy department, he had to be aware of Professor Josiah Royce's teaching that life is the manifestation of the "Absolute," and that reality reflected an "Eternal and Absolute Mind and Will." At the pool-of-light numinous experience at the beginning of "Burnt Norton," Eliot has the mysterious bird, derived with conscious irony from Emerson, say "humankind / Cannot bear very much reality," meaning this powerful metareality. These revelatory experiences constitute the "still point" around which Eliot's verse turns, especially and explicitly after 1930—the world turning around the still point, the turning world consisting of the chaos of ordinary experience. Eliot's quest for divine intuition involves the purification of the senses through discipline, prayer, ritual, waiting, and silence. Eliot gradually saw the intersection of time and eternity as the Incarnation of Christ in Jesus. In the final quartet, "Little Gidding," the pilgrim makes the journey to that remote spot, the tiny chapel still standing and once the site of an Anglican retreat associated with George Herbert and Nicholas Ferrar. At this point, the poem says, "prayer has been valid."

✦

Around his primal insight Eliot built a structure consisting of "tradition" as used in the special sense defined in his essay "Tradition and the Individual Talent" (1919)—the title itself suggesting that the individual's cognition is not enough. As Arnold had said, the Protestant principle is "individual judgment." To that principle Eliot opposes the "historical sense" that "involves a perception, not only of the pastness of the past, but of its presence; the historical sense compels a man to write not merely with his own generation in his bones, but with a feeling that the whole of the literature of Europe from Homer and within it the whole of the literature of his own country has a simultaneous existence and composes a simultaneous order. This historical sense, which is a sense of the timeless as well as of the temporal and of the timeless and of the temporal together, is what makes a writer traditional."

This breathtaking sense of the whole tradition constitutes a structure of always present works of literature and philosophy that sustain and validate Eliot's primal insight and the poetic practice that goes with it. Nothing could be further than this from Frost's Protestant individualism, in which the individual's experience is the sole principle of validation. As has often been said, all political and cultural differences are, at bottom, religious differences.

All of this might usefully be examined from another perspective—that of the sociology of knowledge, especially as regards the knowledge of the metaphysically transcendent. One of the fundamental propositions of the sociology of knowledge holds that the felt plausibility of a view of reality depends upon the social support it receives. We obtain our notions about the world largely from other people, and these notions continue to be plausible to us because others continue to affirm them. The signals of transcendence in Frost are intermittent and tend toward the ambiguous. The consciousness in Frost's poetry, resolutely individualistic, discovers truths on its own and tests them on its own. In terms of the sociology of knowledge, this individual consciousness is secure in affirming what everyone else affirms—the truth of the familiar world of the five senses. That constitutes its "plausibility structure."

Eliot, in contrast, belongs to a supportive cognitive community—only it exists in time rather than in space. Eliot's spatial community, like Frost's, is the ordinary, secularized modern Western world, the fragmented world of *The Waste Land*. But, as Eliot's poetry develops along its Dantean line, his "neighbors" gradually manifest themselves to include Julian of Norwich, Saint John of the Cross, Nicholas Ferrar, George Herbert, Charles I, John Milton, John Donne, and all the others from Homer through the present who constitute the tradition that is always present in Eliot's mind.

Such intimations of eternity as are available through experience to Eliot receive support from this timeless Christian community. As the sociology of knowledge tells us, such support confirms the plausibility of the individual's insight. Frost and Eliot are "elective"—in Goethe's sense of the word, that is, destined—antagonists; though all of the aggression, defensive in its motive, came from Frost.

Late in their lives Eliot tried to bury the hatchet with Frost. In 1947 Eliot appeared unexpectedly at Frost's door on Brewster Street in Cambridge; they had a cup of tea and discussed poetry. In June 1957 Frost visited England, asked to do so by the American government as a goodwill ambassador. He received honorary degrees from Oxford and Cambridge, as well as many other honors and toasts, and on June 17 he was a guest of the English-Speaking Union. Eliot introduced him, saying gracefully and accurately, "You know, as one gets older, one cares less about movements and tendencies and groups. We all have our own idiom and metric and subject matter, but I have come to feel that there are only two kinds of poetry—good and bad. And the bad poetry can be very much of one's own type, and the good poetry can be of a very different type. . . . Mr. Frost is one of the good poets, and I might say, perhaps the most distinguished, I must call it, poet now writing."[9] The fire and the rose were one.

CHAPTER TWO

F. Scott Fitzgerald: A Capacity for Wonder

Was it a vision, or a waking dream?
Fled is that music: —do I wake or sleep?
      —John Keats, "Ode to a Nightingale"

But yet I know, where'er I go,
That there hath pass'd away a glory from the earth.
      —William Wordsworth, "Immortality Ode"

In the famous passage that concludes *The Great Gatsby*, Fitzgerald recalls the long ago Dutch sailors and their first glimpse of the New World, imagining their "capacity for wonder" in the presence of immense possibility. It is Jay Gatsby's own imagination of possibility and belief in his luminous destiny that associates him with those Dutch sailors and makes him a distinctively American hero.

In *This Side of Paradise* (1920) Fitzgerald reported on the shift away from Victorian manners and mores, notably in the chapter called "Petting." His response to the collapse of Victorian assumptions was romantic intensity, the golden moment.[1]

This Side of Paradise sold forty thousand copies and propelled F. Scott Fitzgerald to a legendary early success. For all its obvious defects, this first novel still possesses energies that make it live. Throughout the 1920s Fitzgerald was a prose poet of the golden moment and the pain of its loss.

At the end of *This Side of Paradise* young Amory Blaine has lost his love, the wealthy Rosalind Connage, because he lacks enough money. He is on his way back to Princeton. "Frost and the promise of winter thrilled him now. . . . Long after midnight the towers and spires of Princeton were visible—with here and there a late-burning light. . . . He stretched out his arms to the crystalline, radiant sky. 'I know myself,' he cried, 'but that is all.'" The reader may wonder what it is he knows about himself after the confusions of his life, the riot of emotions. The answer comes in *The Great Gatsby*. The first time Nick Carraway sees Jay Gatsby he too is stretching out his arms: toward the green light at the end of Daisy Buchanan's dock. Like Amory Blaine, Jay Gatsby is a romantic idealist, and the prisoner of a dream, which is a form of transcendence that for such an idealist provides focus and meaning in life, and desolation when the dream dies.

But being an American in that sense was indeed a "complex fate," in Henry James's phrase. When I think of F. Scott Fitzgerald today I recall in a Proustian moment the circumstances and the single sentence in *This Side of Paradise* that made me suddenly aware of Fitzgerald's own capacity for wonder, and almost simultaneously aware of his ability to communicate that wonder in a distinctive prose.

It's Christmas vacation. As the New York Central train full of college students lurches southward through Massachusetts college towns and frozen Dartmouth recedes northward behind us, the car is full of pipe and cigarette smoke, and whiskey pints go around. Smith girls board at Northampton, Yale men appear at New Haven. Far down the tracks New York beckons. No one thinks the noun *New York* has anything to do with New York State. New York is Manhattan. In the dormitories students have been humming songs from the big Broadway musicals, Eastern Seaboard music. Still far in the future are those redneck adenoidal moans. Now is the golden age of the big Broadway shows, roaring down to us out of the 1920s. The biggest and grandest musical of all, *South Pacific*, is now on Broadway, tickets almost impossible to buy; it's one of the major musicals in the history of that genre, America's special contribution to the theater. Neither the late 1940s nor the entire 1950s were dull, as some later insisted. In fact the 1950s were exciting and had quite a bit in common with the 1920s. Fitzgerald said that there are no second acts in American life, but the 1950s proved him wrong as he once again became a best seller and was rediscovered by the critics.

This night, as New York lies ahead with Christmas just beyond it, the goal of some of us on the train is the lobby of the Biltmore Hotel, across Vanderbilt Avenue from Grand Central Station. Amid cocktail music we will find the legendary meeting place under the famous clock, nestling like a love token in the golden scrollwork of its base. A lot of the girls there will wear camel hair or fur coats, Fair Isle sweaters, loafers. Everyone will be going to dinner, to a movie, to a musical, to parties, to the Plaza or the Stork Club, the jazz joints on Fifty-Second Street or else in the Village. Our train lurches and clatters through the dusk.

I am nineteen, and I have never heard of F. Scott Fitzgerald. The great Fitzgerald boom as yet amounts only to an anticipatory tremor. My father had suggested that I read *This Side of Paradise,* a 1920 college novel from his era, and I have with me a copy from the Dartmouth library, a shabby-looking volume rebound in a sort of oatmeal-colored stuff. Grim. But as I read Fitzgerald's prose the world becomes luminous, beginning with the debonair insouciance of his opening sentence: "Amory Blaine inherited from his mother every trait, except the stray inexpressible few, that made him worth while." A few sentences later, after Amory's weak father has been dismissed, permanently, it turns out that his mother was special: "But Beatrice Blaine! There *was* a woman!" This young writer will have to do something with *that.* He has set the bar high, and will have to deliver. *But Beatrice Blaine! There was a woman!* Given such a bravura introduction, and a mother like that, what were the "inexpressible few" traits Amory did *not* inherit from such a mother that "made him worth while?" I am beginning to be carried along by the language here, its rhythms, surprises, brightness, and constant daring. Paul Valéry wrote that "unconsciously we lend the characters of a novel all the human lives which exist in us potentially." Perhaps that is so. Amory now, and his Princeton, call to me, and Fitzgerald's prose evokes a sympathetic response in my own mind. He also writes of young love, its excitement and its aching disappointments, a subject then of interest to me, and a worthy subject for literature, as Goethe understood so well as I saw later in *The Sorrows of Young Werther*—though not many of us commit suicide as Werther did when love is lost. Amory Blaine just gets blotted out drunk.

More than a decade later, when I was an English instructor at Columbia, Lionel Trilling brought this novel up, smiled his small sweet smile, and said: "I first read that as a Columbia student. I said to myself, 'That's really the way to go to college.' " Trilling was not alone in that feeling. The young John O'Hara, in small town Pottsville, Pennsylvania, read it and dreamed of an Ivy League education. In his introduction to *The Portable F. Scott Fitzgerald,* O'Hara remembers that "half a million other men and women between fifteen and thirty, fell in love with that book."

The year 1945 had a lot in common with the year 1920. The young men had come home from Europe and the Pacific, and once again great things were expected from new writers. John Aldridge reflected on this moment in *After the Lost Generation* (1951), having hoped for much and received but little: Norman Mailer, Truman Capote, Gore Vidal, Frederick Buechner, Paul Bowles, Vance Bourjaily, William Styron, Irwin Shaw,

John Horne Burns, Alfred Hayes. Something had gone wrong. This was not permanent achievement. John Horne Burns's *The Gallery* was probably the best of the lot, but who even mentions it now? The problem might have been that this world war did not have the culturally transforming effect of the earlier one that had finished off the Victorian era and launched the 1920s, the first modern decade.

As it happened, in 1945, after the Lost Generation, that same Lost Generation began to make what would be a big return engagement. With a rush, the 1920s were back. In 1945, the year the war ended, New Directions brought out *The Crack-Up*, a collection of essays by and about F. Scott Fitzgerald, also containing some passages from his notebooks, a few poems by others, and several important letters of appreciation. Edited by Fitzgerald's not-so-friendly friend Edmund Wilson, *The Crack-Up* found its moment, most especially Fitzgerald's bittersweet memories of the Jazz Age: "And lastly from that period I remember riding in a taxi one afternoon between very tall buildings under a mauve and rosy sky; I began to bawl because I had everything I wanted and knew I would never be so happy again. . . . Come back, come back, O glittering and white." *That dying fall, "never be so happy again," is integral to an understanding of Fitzgerald.* But that New York in 1949 was now *our* city. *The Crack-Up* took its place in the Fitzgerald canon and soon became one of *our* books.

Following the attention attracted by *The Crack-Up*, Dorothy Parker edited the previously mentioned Viking edition, *The Portable F. Scott Fitzgerald*. Appearing in 1945, it contained *Gatsby, Tender Is the Night*, and some important stories, but, strangely, some other stories that are far from his best. To quote again from the introduction, O'Hara awards Fitzgerald the compliment of "writing better than any of his contemporaries." Fitzgerald returned to print in a big way during the 1950s, accompanied by a tide of books and essays reflecting critical acclaim and biographical interest, most immediately a biographical and critical study by Arthur Mizener, a novel by Budd Schulberg, and then many other books and articles. Despite Fitzgerald's remark that there are no second acts in American lives, as an author he certainly has had a second act. The sales of *Gatsby* in 2006 reached a quarter of a million copies a year. Cambridge University Press has published Fitzgerald's collected works with complete scholarly apparatus. *Gatsby* continues to be the subject of commentary and is approaching Samuel Johnson's one hundred years of esteem that establishes classic standing. In his essay on Fitzgerald in *The Liberal Imagination* (1950), Lionel Trilling judged that this novel "grows in weight and significance with the years," and observed that Fitzgerald

wrote with the voice of gentleness without softness, an excellent formulation of the effect of his prose, its gentleness expressing awareness of
human weakness and mortality.

During the postwar period, say from 1945 to the late 1950s, literary
young men did not turn with great interest to the new writers of their
own period. Among much else, we rediscovered Fitzgerald. He *was* of
our period. We highly valued the Hemingway of the 1920s and waited,
but his Big Book never arrived. Malcolm Cowley in 1949 performed a
signal critical act in pulling together the Yoknapatawpha saga in Viking's
Portable Faulkner. Frost was a powerful presence, though most of us
underrated him then, while Eliot, more exciting than Frost, or so we
thought, hovered authoritatively somewhere over the mid-Atlantic. We
read Mann, Proust, Joyce, Kafka, Eliot, and Yeats, all of them modernist
masters of distinctive and powerful work, and all of them unmistakably
major. Fitzgerald was a luminous presence among them. We had little
interest in such writers as Steinbeck, Farrell, Richard Wright, and Arthur
Miller—all, for us, *losers,* and dreary, lacking in style and aspiration, like
a row of WPA (Works Progress Administration) post office murals.

On that uproarious yet reasonably innocent train ride toward the
Biltmore clock, I met Fitzgerald in the second paragraph of *This Side
of Paradise.* I had read the usual high school books—Longfellow, Dick-
ens—but he made me pay attention for the first time to what could be
done with words. I read that opening of *This Side of Paradise:* after some
debonair phrases dismissive of Amory's father, a spiritless and wispy man,
Fitzgerald now writes—and let us return to that challenge Fitzgerald sets
for himself as a writer: *"But Beatrice Blaine! There* was *a woman!"* To
set something up that way, a writer commits himself to deliver, much as
Babe Ruth is believed to have called his shot in the 1932 World Series. Of
course, this is the 1920s, when Lindbergh really did take off from Gatsby's Long Island and flew across the Atlantic alone. The impossibly young
Fitzgerald, twenty-four at the beginning of the 1920s, manages to deliver
now the beautiful, grandly wealthy, absurdly spoiled Beatrice Blaine. She
is at once outlandish, comic, and marvelous. If Beatrice Blaine is possible,
anything is possible. The very wealthy Beatrice and young Amory set out
for Europe on an ocean liner:

> However, four hours out from land, Italy bound, with Beatrice, his
> appendix burst, probably from too many meals in bed, and after
> a series of frantic telegrams to Europe and America, to the amaze-
> ment of the passengers the great ship slowly wheeled around and
> returned to New York to deposit Amory at the pier.

Along with possibility, and with that ocean liner straining probability in a Gatsbyan way, there enters another important aspect of Fitzgerald's universe. Things can be scintillating, like stars in the firmament—many will be much more so even than his Beatrice Blaine, but somehow, maybe because of their very quality of iridescence, they are always disappearing into the dark. The golden idea, the pleasure the reader has in Beatrice, gives way to that dying fall rhythm. As we read on the second page of *This Side of Paradise:* "All in all Beatrice O'Hara had absorbed the sort of education that will be quite impossible ever again . . . in the last of those days when the great gardener clipped the inferior roses to produce one perfect bud." There it is: "*impossible ever again,*" stressed-unstressed/unstressed-stressed, dactylic/iambic. Fitzgerald was aware very early of the conjunction between beauty and loss, that dying fall rhythm frequent in his prose. "The sentimental person," he wrote, "thinks that things will last—the romantic person has a desperate confidence that they won't." But before the passing of the beautiful vision, Fitzgerald, beginning with this first novel—now, when he was beginning to develop his characteristic powers—had the ability, as Edmund Wilson put it, "to turn language into something iridescent and surprising." This sensibility drew him to Keats for his richness of language and his powerful conjunction of love and death. As early as his college years he imagined that he too had tuberculosis and would die young. It is Jay Gatsby's "capacity for wonder" that for Fitzgerald constituted his greatness, but the wonder exists under threat from time.

I will cite Lionel Trilling again, for his precise sense of where Fitzgerald stands in the literary tradition:

> What Fitzgerald said about his capacity for ecstatic happiness might have been said by Wordsworth; both men gave a peculiar value to their boyhood and youth as definitive of their whole lives, and perhaps Fitzgerald's theory of emotional bankruptcy, his belief that he had a fixed fund of feeling that he would exhaust derives from a similar theory Wordsworth held. Most of Fitzgerald's literary references are to the Romantic writers, and Wordsworth was a clear figure in his mind. So was Keats, from whose poem about youth growing pale and spectre-thin and dying he takes the title of *Tender Is the Night;* his dominant literary mode is that of "La Belle Dame Sans Merci" ["The Beautiful Lady Without Pity"] and "Lamia."[2]

The presence of Keats in Fitzgerald sometimes approaches reincarnation. In addition to Keats, he also memorized entire passages of Swinburne and Rupert Brooke. Like Keats, Brooke died young—Keats of tuberculosis at twenty-five, buried in the Protestant cemetery in Rome; Brooke at twenty-eight on Easter Sunday 1915 of blood poisoning while on his way to Gallipoli. He is buried on the island of Skyros in the Aegean, and now there really is, as he wrote in a famous sonnet, "some corner of a foreign field that is forever England." Fitzgerald as the young author of *This Side of Paradise* had written poetry imitating these poets and turned some of this poetry into rhythmic prose for his first novel, a love letter to Princeton, a love that stayed with him throughout his life. For example, as he wrote in his 1927 essay "Princeton":

> Looking back over a decade one sees the ideal of a university become a myth, a vision, a meadow lark among the smoke stacks. Yet perhaps it is there at Princeton, only more elusive than under the skies of the Prussian Rhineland or Oxfordshire; or perhaps some men come upon it suddenly and possess it, while others wander forever outside. Even these seek in vain through middle age for any corner of the republic that preserves so much of what is fair, gracious, charming and honorable in American life.[3]

For Fitzgerald, the ideal and romantic emotions he experienced at Princeton also attached to the Golden Girl, who first appears in his fiction as Rosalind Connage in *This Side of Paradise*. She rejects Amory because he does not have the money to support the life her beauty deserves. Rosalind is based largely on Ginevra King, a wealthy beauty from Lake Forest, Illinois, who attended the Westover girls' school in Connecticut. Fitzgerald was in love while at Princeton and never forgot. He imagined, incorrectly, that Ginevra King rejected him because he did not have money.[4] *This Side of Paradise* is episodic and possesses numerous flaws as a novel, yet it retains its vitality, and we can unpack it to find in one form or another the major themes of Fitzgerald's novels and many of his stories. We also see the emergence of his characteristic style, evocative of his romantic vision.

In *This Side of Paradise*, along with central elements that appear in his later and better work, Fitzgerald made his thematic and stylistic signature an original kind of surprise, not only in his running narration and incident but in his prose, appearing as a wild and unexpected quality entirely his own. These surprises create a universe in which anything is possible, and appear early, as in *This Side of Paradise* with Beatrice Blaine's extravagant gestures, for example when the ocean liner turns around in midvoyage and returns to New York because Amory has a ruptured appendix, a

phenomenon suggesting the almost magical power of money. The idea
that *anything can happen* appears often in his prose, as in this from "The
Diamond as Big as the Ritz" (1922):

> St. Midas' School is half an hour from Boston in a Rolls-Pierce
> motor-car. The actual distance will never be known, for no one,
> except John T. Unger, had ever arrived there save in a Rolls-Pierce
> and probably *no one ever will again.* [italics added]

"No one ever will again": Is Fitzgerald there satirizing his own dying falls?

The name Saint Midas for the "most expensive and the most exclu-
sive boys' preparatory school in the world" is wonderful as light satire
directed at the older eastern prep schools; also appropriate here is the
interminable parade of Rolls-Pierce automobiles—no other kind, except
the unmentionable model used by the plebian Unger. Now we read on,
finding much that could never have been anticipated:

> "And diamonds," continued John eagerly. "The Schnitzler-
> Murphys had diamonds as big as walnuts—"
> "That's nothing." Percy had leaned forward and dropped his
> voice to a low whisper. "That's nothing at all. My father has a dia-
> mond bigger than the Ritz-Carlton Hotel."

The extravagance of the imagination here, which is comic, looks forward to the extravagance of *Gatsby* and the link of magic with money. In
"The Diamond as Big as the Ritz" we have twin sisters. Here you need to
know—as Fitzgerald tells us in his essay "Echoes of the Jazz Age"—that
the word *jazz* originally meant sex. The names of the twin girls, Kismine
and Jasmine, must be one reason why "The Diamond as Big as the Ritz"
appeared in Mencken's *Smart Set* at a low fee, rather than in George
Horace Lorimer's munificent but staid *Saturday Evening Post*. With Kismine and Jasmine, Fitzgerald was certainly pushing the limits, but in their
exuberance he and Zelda were testing the limits during the 1920s. So was
Jay Gatsby.

As *Gatsby* begins, Daisy Buchanan has been married to Tom for five
years. This is little or nothing to Jay Gatsby, the magician of change: "'Of
course she might have loved him just for a minute. . . . In any case,' he
said, 'it was just personal.'" Gatsby brushes away her five years; time is a
triviality compared with his commanding vision of romantic possibility,
a vision that far transcends time and her merely "personal" experience of
love for Tom.

To a couple of drunken minor Gatsbys after one of Jay Gatsby's gigantic parties, the loss of a wheel from their auto is just as trivial as Daisy's love for Tom:

> "Put her in reverse."
> "But the *wheel's* off."
> He hesitated.
> "No harm in trying."

Jay Gatsby declares: "Can't repeat the past? Why of course you can!" Gatsby is also drunk, in a way.

In this series of quotations we see that surprise in the language is connected with possibility, sometimes absurdly and comically, sometimes tragically. This is a Gatsbyan world of magic in which anything is supposedly possible, and in which, when reality intrudes, the characters continue to try. The world of this prose is nicely epitomized by what Nick Carraway thinks as he rides over the Art Nouveau Fifty-Ninth Street Bridge into Manhattan, Gatsby driving his magical Rolls chariot: "'Anything can happen now that we've slid over this bridge,' I thought; 'anything at all.'" Even the 1919 World Series can be fixed, as he soon finds out.

Where Fitzgerald found these surprises, readers could only guess. He was a magician like Gatsby, prose his métier. We see what Trilling meant, in this respect and others, when he declared that "in Fitzgerald's work the voice of his prose is of the essence of his success."[5] In the Gatsbyan world of transformation money is one ingredient, with imagination necessary as well. The socially transformative power of money must have been one of the things that disturbed the early Renaissance church when it proscribed the taking of interest. Money transformed society as stable landed wealth never could. In his *Faust,* Goethe has Mephistopheles save a bankrupt kingdom with paper money, and elsewhere I have compared Jay Gatsby with Faust.[6]

Yet some limits do exist. Society itself resists surprise. In America social mobility, to a considerable degree, enables you to invent yourself. James Gatz tests those limits when he invents Jay Gatsby, "Oxford man," and runs up against the realism of Tom Buchanan and the resistance of established wealth.

Wealth and surprise appear in *This Side of Paradise,* as Beatrice Blaine's money makes her surprising gestures possible and is connected with what is remarkable in her life. And Amory's Golden Girl Rosalind Connage does reject Amory because he is "poor." For Fitzgerald money has nothing to do with snobbery and is not material but a catalyst of possibility when used with imagination. Tom Buchanan, a very wealthy man, is untouched by imagination and is a brutal material presence, his wealth not buying him our admiration. *This Side of Paradise* is Fitzgerald's valentine to Princeton, often lyrical with his love. He sees Princeton as aristocratic, poetic, and beautiful, associated in his mind with Oxford and inevitably with wealth. *This Side of Paradise* shows that Fitzgerald had read with attention Compton Mackenzie's 1914 *Sinister Street,* now a largely forgotten novel. Oxford, recalled in Mackenzie's "Dreaming Spires," the title of book 1 in *Sinister Street,* becomes the chapter "Spires and Gargoyles" as Amory Blaine arrives at Princeton in *This Side of Paradise.* The name Amory Blaine is related by rhyme to Mackenzie's hero Michael Fane. Amory derives from Hobart Amory Hare Baker, a handsome Philadelphia aristocrat out of Saint Paul's School, and a natural athlete—a Princeton hockey and football star in the class of 1914—whom Fitzgerald hero-worshipped.

During his first dusk on the Princeton campus, Amory is enthralled by a marching parade of singing undergraduates led by Allenby, the football captain. Fitzgerald's lyrical prose expresses the romantic aura of Princeton as he sees it:

> The great tapestries of trees had darkened to ghosts back at the last edge of twilight. The early moon had drenched the arches with pale blue and weaving over the night, in and out of the gossamer rifts of moon, swept a song, a song with more than a hint of sadness, infinitely transient, infinitely regretful. . . . Now, far down the shadowy line of University Place a white-clad phalanx broke the gloom, and marching figures, white-shirted, white-trousered. . . . [Amory] sighed eagerly. There at the head of the white platoon marched Allenby, the football captain, slim and defiant, as if aware that this year the hopes of the college rested on him, that his hundred-and-sixty pounds were expected to dodge to victory through the heavy blue and crimson lines.

These white-clad undergraduates appear out of a slightly sinister darkness. They are already heading back into it, their echo dying away. Allenby bears the name of Field Marshal Edmund Allenby, famous for his wartime deeds in the Middle East, and although the United States remains neutral for the time being, the war is a presence offstage in this novel. Military names describe the student marchers, "phalanx" and "platoon." Their white shirts recall a famous portrait of the poet and beau ideal Rupert Brooke. The Princeton player Allenby, who is to "dodge" through the "heavy" Harvard and Yale lines, is based on Hobey Baker, now in both the Football and Hockey Halls of Fame; he held the Princeton football scoring record for a single game until Cosmo Iacavazzi broke it in 1964. Baker died in 1918, crashing his mechanically suspect Spad plane in France.[7] Allenby is "slim" and quick, recalling Southern formations such as those of Lee and Jackson and the rest of the doomed Confederacy, compared to the "heavy" armies of Grant, represented by the "heavy blue and crimson lines" of Yale and Harvard. This contrast between Lee and Grant appears again, for example, in *Tender Is the Night*. For Fitzgerald, Princeton had aristocratic Southern qualities.

Today the reader will be surprised by the authority the college universe has for Fitzgerald. But during the 1920s far fewer people went to college than is the case today; the Ivy League colleges had more distinctive personalities and were available as aspects of characterization for a novelist.

In much of Fitzgerald's fiction, and centrally in *Tender Is the Night*, the South represents values that have been tragically lost, though Princeton remains a cultural repository of such values. Fitzgerald came from St. Paul, Minnesota, but he had important Maryland ancestry, including the author of the national anthem, Francis Scott Key, after whom he was named, and Mary Surratt, executed as complicit in the plot to assassinate Lincoln.

Tom Buchanan, a former Yale football player, has a cruel and powerful body, not a slim one like Allenby/Baker. In "May Day," the repellent Philip Dean is a Yale man and snubs his broken down former roommate, the artist Gordon Sterrett, at the Yale Club in New York. The egregious Collis Clay in *Tender Is the Night* also went to Yale, as did Dick Diver, who betrayed the vibrant past of his Virginia ancestors and married into the Warren (rabbit warren) Chicago plutocracy. Chicago, like Yale, possesses particularly negative qualities for Fitzgerald, probably deriving from Fitzgerald's rejection by Ginevra King. Her father, Charles Garfield King, a polo-playing multimillionaire, had gone to Yale, though Fitzgerald had no reason to dislike him. Fitzgerald's animus regarding Chicago reappears in *Tender Is the Night* in the brutal, amoral, and plutocratic—not to mention incestuous—Deveraux (social climber's bogus name) Warren.

Ginevra King herself is central to much of Fitzgerald's fiction, and her presence becomes more important when one keeps in mind the entire oeuvre. She is the ever-present Golden Girl who rejects the hero because he lacks the requisite wealth. The first example is Rosalind Connage in *This Side of Paradise*. Another is Judy Jones, who rejects Dexter Green in "Winter Dreams" (1922), and then Daisy Fay, who rejects young Jay Gatsby to marry Tom Buchanan. It seems that Fitzgerald was completely mistaken in thinking that Ginevra or her family rejected him because he lacked money, although this spectacular mistake pervaded his mind, became a kind of myth, and inspired much of his fiction.

In August 1916, in what seemed brutal and outrageous to Fitzgerald, he was rejected by the beautiful and wealthy Lake Forest (Chicago) debutante. His competitors had been sons of wealth. In August 1916 it supposedly was remarked within his hearing at a party in Lake Forest that "poor boys should not think of marrying rich girls." The importance of this has been stressed by Fitzgerald's biographers.

But James L. W. West III has refocused on Ginevra King in his valuable *Perfect Hour* (2005), based on recently available letters from Ginevra to Scott and on her diaries, an indispensable study for this aspect of Fitzgerald's narrative of himself. It does not look at all as if Fitzgerald, being relatively poor, broke up the romance. He met Ginevra at a party in his hometown of St. Paul on January 4, 1915, and they began an intense romance that flourished for six months and lasted for two years. Though she destroyed Fitzgerald's letters at his request, he saved typewritten transcriptions of hers, no doubt for literary use. From her letters much of the content of his own letters can be inferred. Her letters and diaries afford an especially vivid account of the courtship manners of the period, and of Ginevra herself as a young woman. On January 5, 1915, the day after first meeting Scott, she writes in her diary:

> Am absolutely gone on Scott! Dressed for dinner. Afterwards Jimmie J. and F. Hurley came & got us & took us to Lib MacD. Danced and sat with Scott most all evening. He left for Princeton at 11— oh—! Went for ride in R's car with Bug and J. J. Fun. Home at 12 —— Scott ——!

Because Ginevra went to Westover in Connecticut while Scott was at Princeton, the romance was largely epistolary, though they met whenever it could be managed. "Throughout Ginevra's letters," writes Mr. West, "one finds frequent notes of longing and frustration. She and Scott cannot see each other; they have only letters and photographs. On March 12th, her emotions spill over:

> Oh Scott, *why* aren't we —— somewhere else to-night. Why aren't we at a dance in summer now with a full moon and a big lovely garden and soft music in the distance.

"For the first time," Mr. West comments, "she signs the letter 'Love, Ginevra.' "

The King family entirely approved of young Fitzgerald, as shown by the fact that on a trip east Mrs. King took Ginevra and Scott out for dinner and to some memorable entertainments, as Ginevra records in her diary:

> Up at 5.00—New York at ten. Ma met me and we shopped *hard*
> all day. *Scott* came for dinner which we had on the Ritz roof gar-
> den. . . . "Nobody Home" afterwards. Then to Ziefield's Midnight
> Frolic at New Amsterdam. Bed at *1*—

Mr. West's elucidation of this is important, demonstrating the King family's apparent approval of the young Princeton man:

> The entry needs a little explaining. *Nobody Home* was a popular
> play that was running at the Princess Theater; Ginevra's father had
> bought the tickets for them during a recent trip to New York. *The
> Midnight Frolic*, a show produced by the theater impresario Flo-
> renz Ziegfeld, whose name Ginevra misspells, was a gaudy, leggy
> affair presented nightly in the roof garden atop the New Amster-
> dam Theater on West 42nd Street.

Years later, in July 1932, Fitzgerald remembered that evening, writing in
"My Lost City":

> I took the style and glitter of New York even above its own valu-
> ation. . . . I felt that no actuality could live up to my conception of
> New York's splendor. Moreover she to whom I fatuously referred as
> "my girl" was a Middle Westerner, a fact that kept the warm center
> of the world out there, so I thought of New York as essentially cyni-
> cal and heartless—save for one night when She made luminous the
> Ritz Roof on a brief passage through.

During the last year of his life, Fitzgerald wrote to his daughter Scotty,
"Once I thought Lake Forest was the most glamorous place in the world.
Maybe it was." Those three words remain memorable as a crystallization
of Fitzgerald's sensibility, in his capacity to see Lake Forest, associated
with Ginevra, as a luminous place with romantic feeling remembered
twenty years later.

Nothing in Mr. West's examination of Scott and Ginevra in 1915 and
1916 indicates that Scott was unacceptable to the King family. Rather,
it appears that Ginevra herself became impatient, then angered, by his
persistent efforts to analyze her personality and by his annoying jeal-
ousy. She was not the only person close to Fitzgerald who found this
unacceptable. Later, on the Riviera, Sara Murphy became hotly indig-
nant about Fitzgerald's questions when they trespassed into personal
matters.

Their romance was over by January 1917. Fitzgerald's belief that wealth and station had destroyed their love became an energizing force in his fiction, in novels and a long series of stories inspired by his mistake about what destroyed their relationship.[8] Had he married Ginevra, Mr. King might well have promoted him in the Chicago business world, and, in becoming a wealthy man himself, he might have been lost to literature.

The stories "Absolution" (June 1924) and especially "Winter Dreams" (December 1922) are among Fitzgerald's best and explore the emotional material that would go into *The Great Gatsby* (1925). To my mind, "Winter Dreams" stands among the very best of his stories, exciting as a glimpse of his advance as a writer and for its intrinsic power. It concludes with a prophetic passage, an extraordinary expression of loss when the capacity for wonder disappears. This passage, indeed, was Fitzgerald's favorite passage in all his work, and he recited much of it upon request. Written when Fitzgerald was only twenty-six, this passage expresses with unforgettable power the older Dexter Green's loss of his earlier romantic capacity to experience the golden moment. Only two years after *This Side of Paradise*, Fitzgerald appears to think the romantic capability a highly perishable thing. This passage may be compared with Wordsworth's sense of loss in his "Immortality Ode":

> There was a time when meadow, grove, and stream,
> > The earth, and every common sight,
> > > To me did seem
> > Apparelled in celestial light,
> The glory and the freshness of a dream.
> It is not now as it has been of yore;
> > Turn wheresoe'er I may,
> > > By night or day,
> The things which I have seen I now can see no more.

In "Winter Dreams" Fitzgerald creates the prose that expresses both the visionary moment and the emptiness when that power is gone.

As a boy, Dexter Green, the hero of "Winter Dreams," worked as a caddie at the Sherry Island Golf Club, sometimes caddying for the spoiled child Judy Jones. Socially, Dexter was a cut below the membership, but during the winter he dreams at night over and over again of golfing glory and social success. James Gatz would have such dreams of glory. As a rising young man, Dexter falls in love with Judy Jones, now a wealthy, beautiful, and sought-after girl at the club. Idyllic moments that become part of Dexter's mind occur, as when lying on a raft at night and listening to music across Black Bear Lake, he meets Judy Jones again, having achieved a modest success, but . . . in the laundry business. In this prose we have both the golden moment and a sense of elegy, that is, of the inevitable passing of that moment forever:

> There was a fish jumping and a star shining and the lights around the lake were gleaming. Over on a dark peninsula a piano was playing the songs of last summer and of summers before that—songs from "Chin-Chin" and "The Count of Luxemburg" and "The Chocolate Soldier"—and because the sound of a piano over a stretch of water had always seemed beautiful to Dexter he lay perfectly quiet and listened.
>
> The tune the piano was playing at that moment had been gay and new five years before when Dexter was a sophomore at college. They had played it at a prom once when he could not afford the luxury of proms, and he had stood outside the gymnasium and listened. The sound of the tune precipitated in him a sort of ecstasy and it was with that ecstasy he viewed what happened to him now. It was a mood of intense appreciation, a sense that, for once, he was magnificently attuned to life and that everything about him was radiating a brightness and a glamour he might never know again.

This is the luminous moment, expressed in strong lyrical writing, the lack of subordination in the sentences tending to blend the details into a single beautiful impression. Yet "might never know again," the dying fall, seems ominous. The sensibility shown there persuades us that he deserves the Golden Girl, who appears, or reappears, in the form of Judy Jones. She circles up in her speedboat and invites him to take over while she water-skis behind. His emotions respond intensely to her beauty, which is bound up with this transforming moment and with his own sense of his impending greater success in business. He loves her. She toys with his emotions carelessly and jilts him twice; finally he leaves her and goes east to a still larger success than was likely in Black Bear, Minnesota. Then comes the shattering climax, Dexter's tragedy consisting not of his loss of Judy Jones, but of the loss he has sustained of the power to feel as once he did. The passage may indeed be as powerful as any he ever wrote. On that ground, I will quote it at unusual length. A business acquaintance from Detroit turns up who knows the later Judy Jones: "She was a pretty girl when she first came to Detroit." That she has ended in *Detroit* sounds a flat note. And: "You must have seen it happen. Perhaps I've forgotten how pretty she was at her wedding. I've seen her so much since then, you see. She has nice eyes":

> A sort of dullness settled down upon Dexter. For the first time in
> his life he felt like getting very drunk. He knew that he was laugh-
> ing loudly at something Devlin had said, but he did not know what
> it was or why it was funny. When, in a few minutes, Devlin went
> he lay down on his lounge and looked out the window at the New
> York sky-line into which the sun was sinking in dull lovely shades
> of pink and gold.

He had thought that having nothing else to lose, he was invulnerable at last—but he knew that he had just lost something more, as surely as if he had married Judy Jones and seen her fade away before his eyes.

> The dream was gone. Something had been taken from him. In a sort
> of panic he pushed the palms of his hands into his eyes and tried to
> bring up a picture of the waters lapping on Sherry Island and the
> moonlit veranda, and gingham on the golf-links and the dry sun
> and the gold color of her neck's soft down. And her mouth damp to
> his kisses and her eyes plaintive with melancholy and her freshness
> like new fine linen in the morning. Why, these things were no longer
> in the world! They had existed and they existed no longer.
> For the first time in years the tears were streaming down his face.
> But they were for himself now. He did not care about mouth and
> eyes and moving hands. He wanted to care, and he could not care
> . . . and there was no beauty but the gray beauty of steel that with-
> stands all time. Even the grief he could have borne was left behind
> in the country of illusion, of youth, of the richness of life, where his
> winter dreams had flourished.
> "Long ago," he said, "long ago, there was something in me, but
> now that thing is gone. Now that thing is gone, that thing is gone.
> I cannot cry. I cannot care. That thing will come back no more."

Prose does not get much better than that, its rhythms perfectly reflect-ing the movement of feeling. The passage switches from outer detail to inner reaction with the sentence "He knew that he was laughing loudly at something Devlin had said, but he did not know what it was or why it was funny." In its cadence, Fitzgerald's lyrical gift has never been more sure. But, with Wordsworth, he was understanding that a time could come when "there hath passed away a glory from the earth." Fitzgerald seems aware that he has written for the Golden Girl, worked for her, and that his powers are connected with her. Her very possibility made his world iridescent. Perhaps Jay Gatsby, had he not been murdered, would have celebrated somehow, if only in his mind, his lost dream of Daisy, as Fitzgerald did celebrate Ginevra. Indeed, Gatsby in fact possessed the gift of surprising language. He passes this on to Nick, who, before knowing Gatsby, would have been incapable of the prose aria about Dutch sailors and infinite possibility that ends the book:

> Most of the big shore places were closed now and there were hardly any lights except the shadowy, moving glow of a ferryboat across the Sound. And as the moon rose higher the inessential houses began to melt away until gradually I became aware of the old island here that flowered once for Dutch sailors' eyes—a fresh, green breast of the new world. Its vanished trees, the trees that had made way for Gatsby's house, had once pandered in whispers to the last and greatest of all human dreams; for a transitory enchanted moment man must have held his breath in the presence of this continent, compelled into an aesthetic contemplation he neither understood nor desired, face to face for the last time in history with something commensurate to his capacity for wonder.

His experience of Jay Gatsby has transformed Nick. This is not the young man of the opening who admires such a bromide as this handed to him by his father: "Whenever you feel like criticizing anyone . . . just remember that all the people in this world haven't had the advantages you've had."

That *The Great Gatsby* possesses important elements that make it a classic in the modernist mode is not generally understood. Now, in 1925 Fitzgerald breaks out of a cocoon as a larva becomes a butterfly, finding models of the highest quality. For *This Side of Paradise* he had looked to Compton Mackenzie and the H. G. Wells of *Tono-Bungay*; next, for *The Beautiful and Damned* (1922), he reflected pessimistic naturalists such as Frank Norris. For *Gatsby,* his acute artistic sense responding to what could advance his art, he had learned indispensable lessons from Conrad and Eliot. Yet he understands his strengths and the continuities with his own material.

In December 1925, T. S. Eliot wrote to Fitzgerald about *Gatsby:*

I have, however, now read it three times. . . . It has interested and
excited me more than any new novel I have seen, either English or
American, for a number of years.

When I have time I should like to . . . tell you exactly why it
seems to me such a remarkable book. In fact it seems to me to be
the first step that American fiction has taken since Henry James.

By 1925, the author of *The Waste Land* had achieved enormous prestige
in the world of high culture; it is not surprising that Fitzgerald carried this
letter in his pocket to show to those who would understand its importance, and even to strangers who happened to recognize him and asked
for an autograph.

From Conrad's *The Nigger of the Narcissus* (1897) and *Heart of
Darkness* (1902), Fitzgerald had learned the uses of the partially involved
first-person narrator, a device that permits the selectivity and concentration lacking in Fitzgerald's first two novels. As Conrad's Marlow is to Mr.
Kurtz, Nick Carraway is to Jay Gatsby, reliable observers gradually moving us closer to the improbable man of extremes.

Both Kurtz and Gatsby in Conrad's phrase are men who have "kicked
loose of the earth." Gatsby's romantic intensity makes him believe that
he can abolish time, and when he says that Daisy's love for Tom was just
personal, he gives his own passion a universal dimension. Of course he
believes that a man such as he can "repeat the past."

Heart of Darkness is a canonical modernist work, and Mr. Kurtz stands
darkly at the threshold of a dark century, adumbrating its monstrous
crimes, but also its brilliance. His Congo "Inner Station" is the abode of
the darkness of the human heart. Kurtz is a modern *artist*—Rimbaud,
certainly, not the well-meaning Albert Schweitzer—and has immersed
himself in the destructive element. Like Gatsby, a hero of the furthest
extreme, another man on the edge, Kurtz has an intensity that Marlow
cannot approach, except through him. Similarly, Nick Carraway's emotions are tepid compared with Gatsby's and are banal until the final page,
where he is stung into the eloquence of his Dutch sailors' aria by his own
full response to Gatsby, now dead. Along with Daisy and Myrtle, Carraway belongs among the botanical growths of Gatsbyland, a mere seed
that does not flower until the final page.

Fitzgerald studied *The Waste Land* (1922) while he was working on
Gatsby (1925). Everyone was talking about *The Waste Land,* which
was almost immediately seen as a banner of the modernist movement.
Fitzgerald had a superb literary intelligence, even though he was sketchily

educated, and he understood what *The Waste Land* constitutes and what possibilities it had for him. He went so far as to call his valley of ashes, a Flushing Meadows landfill, the "waste land." The eyes of the oculist Doctor T. J. Eckleburg look out over the waste land and, like blind Tiresias in *The Waste Land,* have "seen it all." The action in the novel moves from spring to the autumn of 1922, with a constant beat of time; throughout we might as well hear "hurry up, please, it's time." Myth, fact, and legend mingle in this realm of "Midas, and Morgan, and Maecenas." On Sunday morning, "while church bells rang in the villages alongshore"— bells reminiscent of St. Mary Woolnoth's that sound plaintively in Eliot's *Waste Land*—the revelers head for Gatsby's bacchanals. Popular music sounds in both the poem and the poetic novel.

Nick visits a version of the epic underworld where he finds Meyer Wolfsheim, the magician who has fixed the 1919 World Series, and who is a false Anchises, the guide for Aeneas in Virgil's underworld. Wolfsheim may have been suggested by Arnold Rothstein, the gambler, whom Fitzgerald had met, but Rothstein was a dandy, not a gargoyle. Wolfsheim, in the underworld of a cellar restaurant, may be Rothstein's soul. The first time Nick visits the Buchanan house and grounds, they are alive with spirits. In Eliot's *Waste Land,* behind any door a corn god may lurk. And at the end Gatsby himself, the god of this world of magic, lies surrounded by dead leaves in his swimming pool—death by water, like the fertility god of the myths. *Gatsby* is full of false fertility, that of Myrtle and Daisy, and Eden at the end, that "fresh, green breast" of the New World, lives in memory and aspiration, not in fact.

Jay Gatsby's quest for Daisy *almost* succeeds, though it amounts to a crazy illusion that could not have survived their marriage. The troubadour sings his song but never marries the Lady in the Tower. Still, at the end, and though Gatsby has been buried in the mud, his moon of romantic possibility rises over Long Island, the spirit of imagination, what Fitzgerald elsewhere called "the willingness of the heart," which he said defines America. Coming out of this book, and remembering that moon, one knows that the great World's Fair of 1939–40 will rise precisely out of this Flushing Meadows wasteland. The theme of that fair was "The World of Tomorrow," conceived of as possibility. With *The Great Gatsby,* Fitzgerald both salutes Eliot and answers him. To Eliot's concluding Sanskrit prayer, Fitzgerald opposes the Gatsbyan moon of imagination and creativity. Influenced by Conrad and Eliot, and also by the use of myth in *The Waste Land, The Great Gatsby* belongs in the modernist canon. One catches one's breath at the beginning of chapter 5 when reading:

> When I came home to West Egg that night I was afraid for a moment
> that my house was on fire. Two o'clock and the whole corner of the
> peninsula was blazing with light, which fell unreal on the shrubbery
> and made thin elongating glints upon the roadside wires. Turning a
> corner, I saw that it was Gatsby's house, lit from tower to cellar. . . .
> As my taxi groaned away I saw Gatsby walking toward me across
> his lawn.
>   "Your place looks like the World's Fair," I said.

   With the exception of Nick, the characters in *The Great Gatsby* do not
develop, and are as irreducible as the characters in a dream, always there,
always known, like Madame Sosostris or the typist or Lil or the "hya-
cinth girl." No wonder Eliot was excited by this novel. In important ways,
Eliot charts Fitzgerald country, though *The Great Gatsby* ends not with a
prayer but with a romantic anthem, and Fitzgerald would not match this
achievement ever again.

Following *Gatsby,* Fitzgerald published *The Rich Boy* (1926), a fine
novella about the emotional impoverishment of the very wealthy Anson
Hunter. The rich "are different from you and me," Fitzgerald says at the
outset. Yes indeed, the Fitzgerald hero is not rich, but a middle-class youth
with "winter dreams" like those of Dexter Green, dreams of beauty and
romance he hopes wealth might bring, a world suffused with visionary
imagination.
   The question remains of whether when he finished *The Rich Boy,*
Fitzgerald might have expanded this seventeen-thousand-word novella
into a novel of some fifty thousand words on the scale of *Gatsby.* Ring
Lardner thought this a possibility. The thought troubled Fitzgerald,
and he told Maxwell Perkins that it would be an impossibility.[9] When
I asked Matthew Bruccoli about this, he said no, Fitzgerald could not
have turned *The Rich Boy* into a novel because he did not know enough
about the very rich to bring such a work off.[10] Plausible, but whatever one guesses—could he have familiarized himself with the Tommy
Hitchcock polo-playing rich on Long Island?—he did not make such an
attempt. Later, while working as a screenwriter in Hollywood, he wrote
to his daughter saying that he wished he had followed the example of
The Great Gatsby and had told himself: "I've found my line—from now
on this comes first. This is my immediate duty—without this I am nothing." That was excellent advice, "my line" meaning the concentration and
wider implication of *The Great Gatsby.*

CHAPTER THREE

Hemingway, Fitzgerald, and
The Sun Also Rises

... the lad in the Rue de Notre Dame des Champs
At the carpenter's loft on the left-hand side going down—
The lad with the supple look like a sleepy panther—
... Veteran out of the wars before he was twenty:
Famous at twenty-five: thirty a master—
Whittled a style for his time from a walnut stick
In a carpenter's loft in a street of that April City.
             —Archibald MacLeish, "Years of the Dog"

Romero had the old thing, the holding of his purity of
line through the maximum of exposure ...
             —Ernest Hemingway, *The Sun Also Rises*

Ernest Hemingway emerged slowly in contrast to F. Scott Fitzgerald, deliberately developing a special style with help from Ezra Pound and Gertrude Stein. Hemingway knew that the nineteenth-century order was gone. The style he carefully evolved expressed a way to live in the world and if necessary to endure it, a style that, at its best, had the same quality Hemingway admired in the bullfighter Pedro Romero, "holding the purity of his line through the maximum of exposure." It was a style aware of danger, despair, and death. The Hemingway moral hero, whether man or woman, uses a minimum of words, especially when under pressure. Associated with Hemingway's style, one always senses pain and death. This style was the opposite of Fitzgerald's lyrical expression of possibility.

But amid the pain and chaos of experience the Hemingway hero finds relief, even a form of redemption, in the "good place." In view of Hemingway's special admiration for *The Adventures of Huckleberry Finn*, this "good place" respite may recall Huck and Jim on their raft as they float idyllically along the Mississippi River. In Hemingway's *In Our Time,* such good places recur in "Cross-Country Snow" and while fishing in the "Big Two-Hearted River." In "Cross-Country Snow" Nick Adams and his friend George are skiing in the Swiss Alps: "The rush and the sudden swoop as he dropped down a steep undulation . . . *plucked Nick's mind out* and left him only the wonderful flying, dropping sensation in his body [italics added]." The following exchange indicates that this experience means much more to Nick than to George. We already know that Nick has been wounded in the war:

> "Maybe we'll never go skiing again, Nick," George said.
> "We've got to," said Nick. . . .
> "We'll go, all right," George said.
> "We've got to," Nick agreed.

One senses desperation in Nick's "We've got to."

Later, in "Big Two-Hearted River," Nick's fishing provides such relief, but Nick refuses to fish further along the river in the swamp because fishing in the swamp would be "tragic." Nick is a man on the edge and needs perfection as a kind of therapy. Toward the end of *The Sun Also Rises,* Jake Barnes finds recovery in fishing with Bill Gorton up in Burguete in Basque Country, a needed relief from the complexities and pain back in Pamplona.

Fitzgerald had a spectacular and even mythic early success with *This Side of Paradise* in 1920, becoming the epitome of golden youth, genius, early success, and the Jazz Age, when everything was possible, and his style was unmistakably his own in that precocious novel, its characteristic rhythms expressing a sense of the potential beauty of life as realized in the iridescent moment, a beauty always threatened by time. Five years after *This Side of Paradise* he produced a masterpiece with *The Great Gatsby.* Hemingway's emergence also possessed a mythic quality, that of the obscure avant-garde artist deliberately, slowly, and with great integrity fashioning a new way of writing. The style he evolved expressed a view of life that was entirely different from Fitzgerald's. Hemingway fashioned a disciplined style, understated and factual and able to control powerful emotion when it threatened to become overwhelming. In Paris, he and his wife, Hadley, lived over a sawmill at 113 rue Notre-Dame-des-Champs off the Boulevard du Montparnasse, and this with his early obscurity and apparent poverty suggested artistic integrity. His publications then were almost private events, clearly experimental ventures. First came *Three*

Stories and Ten Poems, brought out by Robert McAlmon's Contact Publishing Company in Paris in July 1923; it was fifty-eight pages, and they distributed 300 copies. Two of these stories, "Out of Season" and "My Old Man," came forward into the 1925 *In Our Time.* The third story, "Up in Michigan," disappears, as do the poems. Two things about one of the stories Hemingway retained are of the first importance. The subject of "Out of Season" is suicide, the suicide of an apparently desperate man because his opportunity to use his barrier against despair, his professional perfection, temporarily disappears. He becomes helpless against emotions he cannot control. But in the story "Out of Season," his terror remains an undercurrent beneath the surface of Hemingway's prose, never becoming explicit. In *Death in the Afternoon* (1932), Hemingway characterized his stylistic goal with a memorable metaphor:

> If a writer of prose knows enough about what he is writing about he may omit things that he knows and the reader, if the writer is writing truly enough, will have a feeling of those things as strongly as though the writer had stated them. The dignity of movement of an ice-berg is due to only one-eighth of it being above water. A writer who omits things because he does not know them only makes hollow places in his writing.

This method develops great power when it engages the reader in discerning the unstated but often dark emotions that exist beneath the surface of Hemingway's prose. The second early pamphlet, *in our time* (lowercase), consists entirely of eighteen numbered paragraphs. These display examples of the new style he had been fashioning, concentrated and suggestive. This was published by Bill Bird's Three Mountains Press, also in Paris, in January 1924; it was thirty two pages and they distributed 170 copies. The use of lowercase letters for the title *in our time* proclaimed the book an enemy of convention, and this brief exercise was beautifully produced and illustrated by a woodcut portrait of Hemingway by Henry Slater, who happened to be a Princeton friend of Fitzgerald's. Indeed, these two works—the first fifty-eight pages, the second thirty-two pages—seem to be moving toward some vanishing point, as if desiring no readers at all, or only a very few discerning readers, who sensed something new and important. Here is one of the eighteen paragraphs from *in our time*:

> They shot the six cabinet ministers at half-past six in the morning against the wall of a hospital. There were pools of water in the courtyard. There were wet dead leaves on the paving of the

courtyard. It rained hard. All the shutters of the hospital were nailed shut. One of the ministers was sick with typhoid. Two soldiers carried him downstairs and out into the rain. They tried to hold him up against the wall but he sat down in a puddle of water. . . . When they fired the first volley he was sitting down in the water with his head on his knees.

This is much more than a straightforward statement of fact in simple declarative sentences. It can be analyzed like a concentrated poem, full of connections and disturbing suggestions. Those sentences announce to a tiny audience the essence of Hemingway's new style, the emotion evoked by violence, death, and terror, controlled by a disciplined style. The edges of Hemingway's words are cleaned and sharpened by the silence in which the dark emotions exist. A metaphor for this ideal of style can be found in the perfection of Pedro Romero in *The Sun Also Rises* (1926) as he risks mutilation or death in the corrida while "holding . . . his purity of line through the maximum of exposure." This represented something entirely new in American literature, and Hemingway began to be a hero of art in advanced literary circles in Paris. Hemingway's innovative style followed the important principle Pound had set forth in *Patria Mia*. Words matter. But often silence is more eloquent.

Edmund Wilson reviewed both of these obscure pamphlets in *The Dial* (October 1924) and made them famous in American literary circles. Facsimile editions of both have been published, and reading the 1924 *in our time* still produces the sense of discovery and excitement aroused by coming upon something entirely fresh and new. As Wilson noticed,

> Mr. Hemingway's poems are not particularly important but his prose is of the first distinction. . . . The characteristic of this school is a naïveté of language often passing into the colloquialism of the character dealt with which serves actually to convey profound emotions and complex states of mind. It is a distinctively American development in prose . . . which has artistically justified itself at its best as a limpid shaft into deep waters.

Writing in Paris, with the understanding and advice of Gertrude Stein and Ezra Pound, who now seems to be a ubiquitous influence, Hemingway had worked slowly to fashion his distinctive new style, at first an effort to write "one true sentence," then building on that toward paragraphs—such as the one about the cabinet ministers, paragraphs concentrated with implied meanings—and making a complex whole when used in the short stories for his first book, *In Our Time* (1925), published by Boni and Liveright, a mainstream publisher in New York.

In *This Side of Paradise* (1920) Fitzgerald presented himself as a mainstream writer and had looked back to a prewar model, Compton Mackenzie's *Sinister Street* (1914), and to prewar Rupert Brooke and also to Keats. Hemingway, who had been wounded in Italy and was living in Paris, a center of modernism, understood how much the war had changed everything, and he began writing with the understanding that earlier literary models were useless. The nineteenth century had been blown to bits. And with great effort he slowly shaped a new style.

In Our Time is a substantial achievement, Hemingway's stories separated by his earlier italicized vignettes, now numbered with roman numerals and called "chapters." The book presents a jagged look as italicized chapters alternate with short stories, but unstated connections exist throughout. The reader senses these connections and gradually understands how they ramify and ultimately involve the central figure in the book, a young American named Nick Adams, even though he is not present in most of the chapters. In its jagged and disconnected form that deeply engages the reader in discovering the thematic connections and deeper meanings, the 1925 *In Our Time* has much in common with *The Waste Land*, as it requires the reader to discern unstated relations among its parts.

In Our Time is not quite a novel but much more than a collection of short stories because it becomes, as the reader proceeds through it, a thematically organized whole. It belongs among Hemingway's most important novels, to be compared in importance with *The Sun Also Rises* (1926) and *A Farewell to Arms* (1929).

In Our Time begins with "On the Quai at Smyrna," neither a story nor an italicized chapter, but an overture announcing the themes that organize the book. "On the Quai at Smyrna" epitomized "our time" of war, atrocity, suffering, and death. Here an anonymous narrator, evidently a British naval officer, describes the scene as the Turks are forcibly and brutally evacuating Greeks from Asia Minor:

> The strange thing was, he said, how they screamed every night at midnight. I do not know why they screamed at that time. We were in the harbor and they were all on the pier and at midnight they started screaming. We used to turn the searchlight on them to quiet

them. That always did the trick. We'd run the searchlight up and down over them two or three times and they stopped it. One time I was senior officer on the pier and a Turkish officer came up to me in a frightful rage because one of our sailors had been most insulting to him.

"On the Quai at Smyrna" provides a thematic entry not only to *In Our Time* but to our own time. Here the terrified Greeks are temporarily quieted by the British searchlight that suggests complete indifference to their suffering and terror. The "frightful rage" of the Turkish officer over insult from a British sailor is out of place, even bizarre, amid what his soldiers are doing to the terrified Greeks. In retrospect this indifference is recognizable as characteristic of much in our time. Need one mention the Nazi extermination camps?

Those screams, heard and unheard, become a pervasive presence in *In Our Time* and forward into our own time. Next we come to chapter 1:

> Everybody was drunk. The whole battery was drunk going along the road in the dark. We were going to the Champagne. The lieutenant kept riding his horse out into the fields and saying to him, "I'm drunk, I tell you, *mon vieux*. Oh, I am so soused." We went along the road all night in the dark and the adjutant kept riding up alongside my kitchen and saying, "You must put it out. It is dangerous. It will be observed." We were fifty kilometers from the front but the adjutant worried about the fire in my kitchen. It was funny going along that road. That was when I was a kitchen corporal.

Terror, again, pervades this. The lieutenant is drunk, the whole battery is drunk, the adjutant is irrationally afraid that the kitchen fire will be seen by the enemy. They are drunk because they are terrified. Like "On the Quai at Smyrna" this is recognizably part of "our time," with violence, death, terror, and, here, drunkenness as one way of facing them. Screams and how to face them has become central to this book.

Peacetime in the United States is not immune to pain, fear, uncontrollable emotion, suicide as the way out. After chapter 1 comes one of the best short stories Hemingway ever wrote, the five-page "Indian Camp." Here Nick Adams, a young boy, accompanies his father, a physician, and his uncle George across a lake in the dark to an Indian camp where the doctor must help an Indian woman having a difficult childbirth. Nick's father must perform a difficult cesarean without anesthetic. Of course she screams. Her husband waits quietly in an upper bunk.

"Oh, Daddy, can't you give her something to make her stop screaming?" asked Nick.

"No. I haven't any anaesthetic," his father said. "But her screams are not important. I don't hear them because they are not important."

The doctor's professional discipline controls his response to the screams. At the conclusion of the successful delivery, the doctor feels understandable professional pride:

"That's one for the medical journal, George," he said. "Doing a Caesarian with a jack-knife and sewing it up with nine-foot, tapered gut leaders. . . . Ought to have a look at the proud father. They're usually the worst sufferers in these little affairs," the doctor said. "I must say he took it all pretty quietly."

"Took it all pretty quietly" indeed. Nick's father is still in his professional mode, talking about "proud fathers" as if he were in his hospital back in civilization. Then comes the shattering fact:

He pulled back the blanket from the Indian's head. His hand came away wet. He mounted on the edge of the lower bunk with the lamp in one hand and looked in. The Indian lay with his face toward the wall. His throat had been cut from ear to ear. The blood had flowed down into a pool where his body sagged the bunk. His head rested on his left arm. The open razor lay, edge up, in the blankets. . . . Nick, standing in the door of the kitchen, had a good view of the upper bunk when his father, the lamp in one hand, tipped the Indian's head back.

Screams, darkness, terror—as in "On the Quai at Smyrna"—briefly and only partially controlled by the doctor's discipline and skill, ending with . . . suicide. (The reader might try to imagine what takes place in our hospitals, out of sight, dealt with through professional discipline and anesthetics.) Virgil famously wrote in the *Aeneid*, "sunt lacrimae rerum," translated as "there are tears at the heart of things"—"things" meaning everything. For Hemingway there are screams at the heart of things especially in our time. In one way or another, most of the chapters and stories in this book deal with terror, screams, and ways of holding them at bay.

At the end of "Indian Camp" Nick's father is rowing back across the lake with Nick in the boat, the father protective but unable to answer Nick's questions that, indeed, are unanswerable:

"Why did he kill himself, Daddy?"

"I don't know, Nick. He couldn't stand things, I guess."

"Do many men kill themselves, Daddy?"

"Not very many, Nick."

"Is dying hard, Daddy?"

"No, I think it's pretty easy, Nick. It all depends."

Nick is still innocent, but asking large questions. Is there a suggestion here that his father is somehow inadequate? Clearly he wishes to be silent. What is there to say? But silence is not adequate as a response to a boy. That these questions occur to the reader suggests how effectively Hemingway has pulled the reader into the situation. Here Nick is still protected by his father, who rows the boat toward home, the story ending on an Edenic note:

> They were seated in the boat, Nick in the stern, his father rowing. The sun was coming up over the hills. A bass jumped, making a circle in the water. Nick trailed his hand in the water. It felt warm in the sharp chill of the morning.
>
> In the early morning on the lake sitting in the stern of the boat with his father rowing, he felt quite sure that he would never die.

As Hazlitt had said in his essay "On the Feeling of Immortality in Youth," "No young man believes he will ever die. . . . To be young is to be with the immortals." With terror and suicide the subject of Hemingway's first story in this book, the reader cannot help thinking of Hemingway's own suicide in 1961. Like the Indian in the upper bunk, "he couldn't stand things," as Nick's father says. Almost immediately in the sequence of chapters and stories, Nick Adams learns that he will suffer and die.

This knowledge becomes a fact of his experience in a constellation that illustrates how this book works as a thematic whole, with stories alternating between chapters. For example, chapter 5, describing the execution of the six cabinet ministers, ends this way: "One of the ministers was sick with typhoid. . . . When they fired the first volley he was sitting down in the water with his head on his knees." Next comes the story "The Battler," which begins, "Nick stood up." Young Nick had been riding illegally on a freight train, now going away from home and into the world. He has been knocked off the train by a brakeman and had a black eye (his first wound). In this story "The Battler," the title could refer to both Nick with his black eye and the punch-drunk—violent and suicidal—former prizefighter Ad

Francis, Nick's doppelgänger in the story. Next comes chapter 6, which makes it explicit that Nick is a "battler" and also mortal:

> Nick sat against the wall of the church where they had dragged him to be clear of machine-gun fire in the street. Both legs stuck out awkwardly. He had been hit in the spine. His face was sweaty and dirty. . . . Up the street were other dead. . . . Nick turned his head carefully and looked at Rinaldi. "*Senta* Rinaldi. *Senta.* You and me we've made a separate peace." Rinaldi lay still in the sun breathing with difficulty. "Not patriots."

But is there a "separate peace"? *In Our Time* tells the reader there is no lasting peace, and no separate peace, only discipline and courage to endure, with temporary relief through pleasures of various kinds and moments of idyllic peace in what Hemingway called a "good place." In "Cross-Country Snow" Nick Adams experiences one such "good place" when skiing in the Swiss Alps with his friend George:

> The rush and the sudden swoop as he dropped down a steep undulation in the mountain side plucked Nick's mind out and left him only the wonderful flying, dropping sensation in his body. He rose to a slight up-run and then the snow seemed to drop out from under him as he went down, down, faster and faster.

This means much more to Nick than it does to his friend George:

> "Maybe we'll never go skiing again, Nick," George said.
> "We've got to," said Nick. "It isn't worth while if you can't."
> "We'll go, all right," George said.
> "We've got to," Nick agreed.

We understand that Nick has been wounded in the war and is a man on the edge. He needs the relief, the therapy, of the "good place." Finally in this book, another good place for Nick is fishing in the "Big Two-Hearted River," the subject of the long story at the end of *In Our Time*. The urgency of fishing here is indicated by the fact that Nick will not as yet attempt to fish in the difficult swamp. It would be *tragic*, he thinks. He must control the experience if it is to have the redemptive effect.

Fitzgerald reviewed *In Our Time* in the *Bookman*, carefully describing the stories and the italicized vignettes (chapters) positioned between them and offering evaluations. Fitzgerald's praise could not have been more enthusiastic:

> I read it with the most breathless unwilling interest I have experienced since Conrad first bent my reluctant eyes upon the sea, . . . [I] have felt a sort of renewal of excitement at these stories wherein Ernest Hemingway turns a corner into the street.

Fitzgerald proceeded to help Hemingway improve his professional situation by helping him move from Boni and Liveright by recommending him to his own editor, Maxwell Perkins, at the more prestigious Scribner's. Fitzgerald's discernment and generosity remind us of Pound's similar efforts with promising poets, the two established writers valuing literature itself more than fearing the possibility of rivalry.

Hemingway's response was surprising. Where gratitude might have been expected, in 1926 he began a quarrel with Fitzgerald that first took the form of an attack in *The Sun Also Rises* and lasted through his treatment of Fitzgerald in the posthumously published *A Moveable Feast* (1964).

This quarrel was literary, ethical, and personal. The ethical aspect of their quarrel was expressed in their contrasting prose styles. Fitzgerald's intense romantic moments, his "capacity for wonder," are reflected in rhythmic, even operatic, Keatsian song. Edmund Wilson observed in a 1922 article that "Fitzgerald is partly Irish," and that "he brings both to life and to fiction certain qualities that are not Anglo-Saxon." Hemingway's prose at its best during the 1920s cleans its edges with silence and is characterized by discipline and the will to make every word count. Under pressure, it finds silence the only ethical way to deal with situations in which, to quote Pound, "words scarcely become a man." Hemingway's prose, influenced by Pound and Gertrude Stein, was moving in a new and modernist direction, while Fitzgerald was bringing forward from the Romantic tradition what expressed his own experience as a twentieth-century writer, and at the same time learning what he could from contemporary modernist authors, including Conrad and Eliot. Hemingway's personal animus toward Fitzgerald certainly came from personal ambition. He had none of Fitzgerald's magnanimity, and as an author, Fitzgerald was the heavyweight champion. And there can be only one heavyweight champion.

When Hemingway's highly original *In Our Time* appeared in October 1925, he would have had reason to think that he had surpassed

Fitzgerald's *This Side of Paradise* (1920) with its prewar models, and *The Beautiful and Damned* (1922), which followed the established realist mode. Though he had surpassed Fitzgerald's first two novels, *The Great Gatsby* changed the entire situation.

Hemingway composed *The Sun Also Rises* with astonishing speed, completing a first draft between July 21 and September 21, 1925, perhaps driven by his fury at having to compete now with *The Great Gatsby*. An important expression of that competition was Hemingway's description of Robert Cohn in *The Sun Also Rises*. Robert Cohn was based on Harold Loeb, but Hemingway's portrait of Cohn often glances at Fitzgerald. The novel begins, "Robert Cohn was once middleweight boxing champion of Princeton. . . . He cared nothing for boxing, in fact he disliked it, but he learned it painfully and thoroughly to counteract the feeling of inferiority and shyness he had felt on being treated as a Jew at Princeton." Fitzgerald had been a Catholic at Presbyterian Princeton. Edmund Wilson recalled that Fitzgerald had been the only literate Catholic he had ever met. Wilson remembered Loeb was outraged when he read this novel, claiming that he had nothing in common with Cohn. He was probably right, because in the novel Hemingway, though with Loeb in mind, attributed to Cohn characteristics that applied more obviously to Fitzgerald. Robert Cohn is a romantic, makes a fool of himself over Brett Ashley, is an aspiring novelist, and admires sentimental novels. This corresponds with Hemingway's view of Fitzgerald. Hemingway regarded Fitzgerald as a romantic who was bad with women because he was sentimental rather than realistic. It seems clear that the Robert Cohn of the novel was an attack on Fitzgerald using Harold Loeb as background.

It must have been embarrassing to Hemingway that Fitzgerald read *The Sun Also Rises* in typescript, because he greatly improved its opening. Hemingway, staying near the Fitzgeralds and the Gerald and Sara Murphys at Juan-les-Pins on the Riviera, showed Fitzgerald a carbon copy of the typescript, only to be humiliated as a craftsman when Fitzgerald, while excited by the novel, advised drastic cuts. Those included the first twenty typescript pages about the earlier life of Robert Cohn and further biographical cuts from the earlier lives of Brett Ashley and Mike Campbell. Fitzgerald, *il miglior fabbro* (the better craftsman), now lectured Hemingway sternly:

> When so many people can write well & the competition is so heavy I can't imagine how you could have done these first 20 pps. so casually. You can't *play* with people's attention—a good man who has the power of arresting attention at will must be especially careful.

Hemingway, so conscious a craftsman as he was, must have been stung by the accuracy of Fitzgerald's advice. These cuts and lesser but still important corrections had to be made in New York, where the book was being processed at Scribner's. With his editing, Fitzgerald had reintroduced Hemingway to his own iceberg principle, leaving out what the reader would sense even if not articulated.

Jake Barnes, an American newspaperman in Paris, the first-person narrator of *The Sun Also Rises,* is impotent because of his war wound but still experiences intense sexual desire. Jake's wound and the pain of his unfulfilled sexual desire are at the center of *The Sun Also Rises.* For Jake the wound and his suffering constitute the fate he must endure, corresponding to the screams at the heart of things. Jake usually controls himself with courage and discipline, but often he also needs Brett Ashley's help. Indeed, they sustain each other. Jake's wound also has wider implications. This war wound resonates as the wound the war dealt to Western civilization. With *The Waste Land* in mind, Jake can be seen as the wounded Fisher King whose wound renders the land sterile, a desert where the crops (lilacs) cannot grow. But there is no Grail in *The Sun Also Rises,* only endurance as Jake and Brett sustain each other.

The exact nature of his wound is one of those omitted facts of which the reader senses the presence, but here cannot quite specify. Yet the question of the wound remains a presence, is there, unanswered, and irritatingly, even excruciatingly, there. That the effect of Jake's wound is visible we learn when he looks at himself in a mirror:

> Undressing, I looked at myself in the mirror of the big armoire beside the bed. . . . Of all the ways to be wounded. I suppose it was funny. I put on my pajamas and got into bed.

The tensions between Jake and Brett resulting from the wound appear early in the novel:

> We stood against the tall zinc bar and did not talk and looked at each other. The waiter came and said the taxi was outside. Brett pressed my hand hard. I gave the waiter a franc and we went out. "Where should I tell him?" I asked.
>
> "Oh, tell him to drive around."
>
> I told the driver to go to the Parc Montsouris, and got in, and slammed the door. Brett was leaning back in the corner, her eyes closed. I sat beside her. The cab started with a jerk.

"Oh, darling. I've been so miserable," Brett said.

This exchange develops the implications of the undefined wound, its nature becoming for the reader a painful and repeated aggravation, and the wound of course is the reason, or main reason, why Brett is "so miserable." The nature of the wound remains the part of the iceberg that remains beneath the water, and, because undefined, becomes the more powerful presence. It also becomes a large metaphor about the ramifying effects of the war on the civilization of the West. *The Sun Also Rises,* however, is more about Brett than Nick. Her toughness, her coarseness, suggest veteran promiscuity. She is a new kind of heroine, with her clipped upper-class British "what rot!" and her realism, her man's felt hat, gender ambiguous name, and short haircut. Perhaps these make her more attractive, and she insists on her sexual freedom. Though Brett derives from Lady Duff Twysden, Hemingway's character may also owe something to Iris Storm in Michael Arlen's immensely popular 1924 novel *The Green Hat.* Iris Storm says twice, accurately, "I am a house of men." Fitzgerald and Hemingway had discussed Arlen's novels, and as Fitzgerald later said, Iris Storm showed that "glamorous English ladies are often promiscuous."[1]

Nothing could be further from Fitzgerald's chaste Golden Girls. Brett has to deal with her powerful sexual urges, no doubt the more exigent because of Jake's incapacity, and she satisfies her sexual hunger first perhaps with Count Mippipopolous in Paris, who has arrow wounds and is "one of us," she says; then with Robert Cohn in San Sebastián just before the scene shifts to Pamplona; and then with the young torero Pedro Romero. Though she and Jake love and sustain each other, she is the one who makes the moral choice in finally tearing herself away from Romero. Brett has a kind of honor and has risked corrupting the young man's pursuit of artistic perfection. "You know," she tells Jake, "it makes one feel rather good deciding not to be a bitch." She feels rather good in giving up Romero. Jake replies with a "yes," the tone of which we can guess:

> "Yes."
> "It's sort of what we have instead of God."
> "Some people have God," I said. "Quite a lot."
> "He never worked very well with me."
> "Should we have another Martini?"

That last line changes the subject while not changing it: they have hit a stone wall. There is nothing more to say. The differences between Jake and Brett there are important. For her, choices are made by the individual alone, in that sense a Nietzschean for whom God is dead, but her aspirations fall short of Nietzsche's lofty imperatives and rise only to doing the right thing. Jake, a Catholic of sorts, tries to pray, but cannot. Whether this is connected with his war wound or to the comprehensive wound the war has caused in the West, we cannot say, though perhaps they are the same thing for this novel. Brett has no sense of God, even at an unreachable distance, and we understand that Brett has been obedient to honor only temporarily. Yet Brett rises above the Lost Generation through her moral choice, which, for her, in her situation, has a kind of tragic heroism, while Jake is a lesser hero whose virtue, impressive too, is stoic endurance.

Throughout *The Sun Also Rises,* both in France and Spain, there are suggestions of the rich past of Europe, established early in the resonant names of Paris streets and boulevards, as in this passage from chapter 4:

> I went out onto the sidewalk and walked down toward the Boulevard St. Michel, passed the tables of the Rotonde, still crowded, looked across the street at the Dome, its tables running out to the edge of the pavement. . . . The Boulevard Montparnasse was deserted. Lavigne's was closed tight, and they were stacking the tables outside the Closerie des Lilas. I passed Ney's statue standing among the new-leaved chestnut trees in the arc light. There was a faded purple wreath leaning against the base. I stopped and read the inscription: from the Bonapartist Groups, some date; I forget. He looked very fine, Marshal Ney in his top-boots, gesturing with his sword among the green new horse-chestnut leaves. My flat was just across the street, a little way down the Boulevard St. Michel.

Jake's senses are alive, enhancing him as the narrator, and that responsiveness contributes to his suffering. Though Jake is a bit sketchy on his French history, the busy and attractive Parisian present mixes with the French past represented most recently by Napoléon's Marshal Ney, a heroic figure who commanded the rear guard of the Grand Army during Napoléon's retreat from Moscow. But the withered wreath and the contemporary Bonapartists suggest a lesser France than was represented by the great marshal. The Catholic presence remains in the names of such streets as the Boulevard St. Michel (St. Michael). Jake has an Old Testament name (Jacob); Brett is a pagan. But the two cannot join in the Western Jerusalem-Athens synthesis. Circe, who turns men to swine as Brett does, yearns for Odysseus, but can never have him. Jake is a wounded Fisher King, but the Grail is broken and this novel is crowded with wastelanders. Hilaire Belloc said, "The faith is Europe and Europe is the faith." In *The Sun Also Rises*, that is possible but highly problematical, since the wound is at the foundation of things.

On hand for the annual Fiesta de San Fermín in Pamplona—the corrida and the saint's name, San Fermín, combining the pagan (archaic Crete) and Christian pasts—the circle around Jake and Brett is a pretty nasty lot, Cohn still believing that his earlier interlude with Brett at San Sebastián actually meant something, while the others understand the emptiness of almost everything. Cohn annoys them by hanging around lovesick as if he had a claim on Brett, with her fiancé Mike Campbell resenting Cohn and insulting him, while Jake and Brett, though in love, are paralyzed sexually by Jake's wound. Hemingway here is indeed fishing the swamp, as Nick promised to do in "The Big Two-Hearted River" at the end of *In Our Time*.

The animus Hemingway directs at Fitzgerald in his account of Robert Cohn is obvious. Like Fitzgerald, Cohn has gone to Princeton, then a citadel of the WASP aristocracy, as has already been noted here. Cohn tries unsuccessfully to be a gentleman, another comment directed at Fitzgerald, not quite a WASP gentleman, even as Jay Gatsby counterfeited a gentleman and was an "Oxford man," though not really one. Adding the British suffix *by* to *gat* does not make it any less a gun. Fitzgerald romanticized sports figures at Princeton; Cohn, a middleweight boxing champion there, has had his nose unromantically flattened in the ring (where Hemingway claimed *heavyweight* skills). We are informed by Jake the narrator that this flattening might have improved a Jewish nose. The "punch in the nose" has a metaphorical quality here. Cohn has bad manners, and is bad with women, that is, romantic and unrealistic, which was Hemingway's contemptuous opinion of Fitzgerald. This is illustrated in the posthumous *A Moveable Feast*, especially in the notorious chapter "A Matter of Measurements," where Hemingway (supposedly) has to reassure Fitzgerald about the size of his penis by taking him to the Louvre and comparing him with nude statues. Fitzgerald's penis, it seems, is adequate. Perhaps the whole episode was a put-on, Fitzgerald kidding the hypermasculine Hemingway. In any case, this use of the Louvre and, say, the *Apollo Belvedere*, is an amusing touch of innocents abroad. Both Cohn and Fitzgerald are sloppy drunks, a violation of good form for Hemingway. Cohn, like Fitzgerald, is a romantic and admires such bad novels as *The Purple Land*, while Jake Barnes, like Hemingway, knows that Turgenev has the right stuff. Cohn, from Hemingway's point of view the worst of all, talks too much. Fitzgerald is present as Cohn in this *roman* à clef, though Harold Loeb, who had thought Hemingway his friend, and was the more obvious model for Cohn, was appalled and furious at his treatment and tried to answer the calumny in his autobiography *The Way It Was*. Hemingway was ruthless and often wounding to his friends, turning on them unexpectedly. Sherwood Anderson had befriended him, and Hemingway had learned from him, as in "My Old Man," though he fiercely denied the obvious influence and savaged Anderson in *The Torrents of Spring*. Fitzgerald could not have failed to notice his presence in Cohn, but never, so far as I know, commented on it, nor did it diminish his regard for Hemingway, his supposed friend, though he objected loudly in 1936, when Hemingway went beyond the acceptable limit in "The Snows of Kilimanjaro," published in *Esquire*. The dying Harry, a writer, thinks about his own rich wife, whom he detests, and then

> remembered poor Scott Fitzgerald and his romantic awe of them and how he had started a story once that began, "The very rich are different from you and me." And how someone had said to Scott, Yes, they have more money. He thought they were a special glamorous race and when he found they weren't it wrecked him just as much as any other thing that wrecked him.

Fitzgerald naturally objected, and in his collected stories Hemingway changed "Scott Fitzgerald" to "Julian."

Hemingway's title *The Sun Also Rises* takes aim at Fitzgerald's moon of romantic possibility, which rises at the end of *Gatsby,* the moon that throughout *Gatsby* reappears, associated with the hero. Keats's nightingale of romance sings its prose arias only in the moonlight, and Jay Gatsby himself always seems much stronger in the dark than in the sunlight. Fitzgerald had read Keats extensively, and had committed to memory large swathes of his verse, and, in addition to "Ode to a Nightingale," would have known about the power of the moon goddess in *Endymion*. Keats's moon sometimes suddenly appears:

> And lo! from opening clouds, I saw emerge
> The loveliest moon, that ever silver'd o'er . . .
> So passionately bright, my dazzled soul
> Commingling with her argent spheres did roll
> Through clear and cloudy, even when she went
> At last, into a dark and vapoury tent.

When Endymion at last meets the moon goddess, she somehow brings the spirit of the moon with her to the bottom of a well as if to protect it from the violations of sunlight:

> When, behold!
> A wonder, fair as any I have told—
> The same bright face I tasted in my sleep,
> Smiling in the clear well. My heart did leap
> Through the cool depth.

The moon often accompanies the appearance of Gatsby. When Nick first sees him it is by moonlight as Gatsby gazes rapturously at Daisy's green light. When Gatsby is bidding farewell to his raucous and far from ideal multitude of guests, "A wafer of a moon was shining over Gatsby's house, making the night fine as before, and surviving the laughter and the sound of his still glowing garden. A sudden emptiness seemed to flow now from the windows and the great doors, endowing with complete isolation the figure of the host, who stood on the porch, his hand up in a formal gesture of farewell." In chapter 6, we learn that Jay Gatsby was born out of James Gatz under the light of the moon: "A universe of ineffable gaudiness spun itself out in his brain while the clock ticked on the washstand and the moon soaked with wet light his tangled clothes upon the floor. Each night he added to the pattern of his fancies." That ticking clock will eventually defeat Gatsby's dream of going back five years to Daisy in 1917. Jay Gatsby seems to flourish at night, weaken, finally lose, and be buried in the daylight. But though Gatsby is dead, his moon rises again over Long Island at the end of the book: "And as the moon rose higher, the inessential houses began to melt away," and out of the valley of ashes in *Gatsby* will rise the New York World's Fair of 1939 40. To be sure, Hemingway's title comes directly from Ecclesiastes: "The sun also ariseth . . . and the wind returneth again according to his circuits. . . . All the rivers run into the sea." Hemingway said that the hero of the book is the everlasting natural word, its permanence and endurance. That is only a partial truth, applying especially to the cleansing trip to Burguete and the trout fishing there: another "good place" like the Big Two-Hearted River. But this celebration of nature and perfect fishing is not the whole mode of moral recovery in this novel, or even the most important, though at Burguete Jake and his friends do find refreshment from the unruly sexual emotions back in Pamplona among Brett, Cohn, Mike Campbell, and Jake. Genuine heroism is defined by Jake and Brett at the end of the book. Hemingway says no to Fitzgerald's romanticism, or, with Lady Brett Ashley, "What rot!" The sun also rises, the sun of moral realism, and with it an appropriate style quite different from Fitzgerald's prose poetry embodying the beauty of the passing golden moment. Brett's best moments are not golden. She apparently is sexually insatiable, and before the fiesta she has even accompanied Robert Cohn for a week in San Sebastián, and later goes off for the same reason with Pedro Romero, the young matador. She is dangerous to men and devours them, though she is the fiancée of Mike Campbell, a broken down and drunken aristocrat. We cannot tell what she might have been had Jake not been wounded. Her tough manner is in part her protection. She has been to the bullring too often, been gored emotionally too often while she gored others, and she has scar tissue, though her toughness can crack.

This novel is in many ways a strange cross-grained object, highly resistant. It strikes us as perverse that this crew of men, all variously in thrall to Brett—the drunk Mike Campbell, the impotent Jake, and the love-sick Cohn—should be sitting around watching *bulls,* the ultimate male symbol, killed in the ring. In a way Campbell and Cohn are steers being gored by Brett, while Jake, permanently a steer, maintains his emotional discipline barely and under pressure. Also aggravating, even during the pre-Hitler 1920s, when country club antisemitism was commonplace, there is nevertheless something sick and beyond the usual in the antisemitism of the little group around Cohn, as if out of weakness they seek a vulnerable target to bully; no doubt the colorful spectacle, the surrounding presence of Spain itself, partially counteracts the grating qualities of this novel. At length, as might have been expected, Brett, Circe-like, draws the young and spotlessly honorable Pedro Romero into her void. Despite or because of the interest of the fiesta and the corrida, and the appeal of the pure, disciplined, and brave Pedro Romero, one increasingly finds Jake's little circle to be a repellent mess. Jake's fishing trip with Bill Gorton to Burguete proves a cleansing antidote, with the Basque countryside, the cheerful Basques, and the squirting leather wine skins, moving up and away from the losers back in Pamplona.

Jake now is in the "good place," here once again in Hemingway, first seen in some of the stories in *In Our Time,* as in "Cross-Country Snow" and "Big Two-Hearted River." In chapter 11 Jake and Bill Gorton are up in Burguete, and Hemingway describes this cleansing experience at persuasive length and with verbal intensity, savoring its details, as its length becomes essential to its power. Even a sample here calls for quotation at some length:

"All right," I shouted. Bill waved his hand and started down the stream. I found the two wine-bottles in the pack, and carried them up the road to where the water of a spring flowed out of an iron pipe. There was a board over the spring and I lifted it and, knocking the corks firmly into the bottles, lowered them down into the water. It was so cold my hand and wrist felt numbed. . . .

While I had him on, several trout had jumped at the falls. As soon as I baited up and dropped in again I hooked another and brought him in the same way. In a little while I had six. They were all about the same size. I laid them out, side by side, their heads pointing the same way, and looked at them. They were beautifully colored and firm. . . .

I walked up the road and got out the two bottles of wine. They were cold. Moisture beaded on the bottles as I walked back to the trees.

Hemingway had said that all that was valuable in the American novel came from *Huckleberry Finn*. He meant Mark Twain's language, the idyll on the raft as Huck and Jim drift down the Mississippi, and the end, where, getting away from the Widow Douglas, or civilization, Huck lights out for the territory, the vast land not yet civilized as states of the Union. In *The Sun Also Rises*, Jake and Bill have lit out to the fishing at Burguete, here a place both a temporary version of Huck's raft and a temporary unspoiled "territory."

Hemingway builds into *The Sun Also Rises* much that Mark Twain did not have, for example, T. S. Eliot. At Burguete, Jake and Bill are *near but not at the monastery of Roncesvalles*. This cleansing of the fishermen (recalling Peter and those other fishermen) also has echoes of *The Waste Land*. Jake, a wounded Catholic Fisher King, cannot pray. Brett is an English Circe, turning men into swine. The Christian (Old Testament) Jacob cannot come together with the pagan Brett to make the Western tradition whole again. Was Circe insatiable, waiting for Odysseus? Eliot's Grail, from the ancient legends involving the cup at the Last Supper and Joseph of Arimathea, is not available here. The fishing trip, a brief idyll, cannot make the wasteland bloom again. Fitzgerald had used *The Waste Land* to advantage in *The Great Gatsby;* now, so powerful was the influence of that poem during the 1920s, Hemingway also uses Eliot, but uses Eliot to compete with *The Great Gatsby*.

To a shared existential crisis, a shared sense of breakdown in the West, Hemingway gives us his own answer. Instead of Eliot's Dantean quest, and in place of Fitzgerald's romantic and creative moon of the imagination at the end of *Gatsby,* Hemingway has something implicit throughout *The Sun Also Rises,* an answer connected with his realism. But first he tortures Jake again when he goes for a refreshing swim at San Sebastián (recalling now Saint Sebastian with the arrows). The arrows sticking in Jake come from that young couple he sees on the raft when he goes for a swim:

> Although the tide was going out, there were a few slow rollers. They came in like undulations in the water, gathered weight of water, and then broke smoothly on the warm sand. I waded out. The water was cold. As a roller came I dove, swam out under water, and came to the surface with all the chill gone.

The slowed pace of the prose, the carefully selected detail, persuade us that Jake's senses are alert; and this prepares us for the pain of what comes next:

> I swam out to the raft, pulled myself up, and lay on the hot planks. A boy and girl were at the other end. The girl had undone the top strap of her bathing-suit and was browning her back. The boy lay face downward on the raft and talked to her. She laughed at things he said, and turned her brown back in the sun. I lay on the raft in the sun until I was dry. Then I tried several dives.

He desperately needs those cooling dives. The slowness of Jake's observations created by his attention to each detail expresses his powerful emotions, and his pain does not have to be made explicit. The reader experiences it. We are sure he will not return to that raft, know he does not belong there with those young lovers. In the emotional logic of the narrative, this soon brings us back to Lady Brett Ashley.

> COULD YOU COME HOTEL MONTANA
> MADRID AM RATHER IN TROUBLE BRETT.

Of course she is in trouble. She always is. Jake soon arrives on the Sud Express: "I saw the Escorial [imperial palace of Philip II] out of the window, gray and long and cold in the sun, and did not give a damn about it. I saw Madrid come up over the plain." What he does give a damn about is Brett. She has left Romero for his own good, and is broke in Madrid. They drink martinis at the Montana bar, and this important exchange is worth repeating here:

"You know it makes one feel rather good deciding not to be a bitch."
"Yes."
"It's sort of what we have instead of God."
"Some people have God," I said. "Quite a lot."
"He never worked very well with me."
"Should we have another Martini?"

For Brett God is dead, while Jake is not so sure. Still, they can come together on one thing they do know. They need each other. That is what counts when one of them is out on the ragged edge. This becomes especially clear when they are at the ragged edge together when *The Sun Also Rises* ends. Now there is nothing more to say. Brett has done the right thing and left Romero, and Jake has rescued her in Madrid. They are together now, have had a tense luncheon together at Botin's, where she cautions Jake not to get too drunk, he having had those martinis at the Montana:

"Don't get drunk, Jake," she said. "You don't have to."
"How do you know?"
"Don't," she said. "You'll be alright."
"I'm not getting drunk," I said. "I'm just drinking a little wine. I like to drink wine."
"Don't get drunk," she said. "Jake, don't get drunk."

She loves Jake and is trying to steady him. He had responded when she needed help. They leave Botin's, a waiter hails a taxi, and they are in fact together now, fragile, and one supposes together only temporarily. Yet this is a powerful love story. They need each other, and those words are too weak, so Hemingway does not try to use words, but he has to deliver here and he does:

The driver started up the street. I settled back. Brett moved close to me. We sat close against each other. I put my arm around her and she rested against me comfortably. It was very hot and bright, and the houses looked sharply white. We turned out onto the Gran Via.
"Oh, Jake," Brett said, "we could have had such a damned good time together."
Ahead was a mounted policeman in khaki directing traffic. He raised his baton. The car slowed suddenly pressing Brett against me.
"Yes," I said. "Isn't it pretty to think so?"

Jake's word *pretty* is realistic, distancing, and precise. That must be the most important traffic cop in the history of literature.

The Sun Also Rises remains a novel that troubles its reader, its hero Jake Barnes sexually maimed, though we are left, annoyingly, to wonder how. The impotent Jake sits there watching bulls being tormented and killed. Meanwhile the woman he loves has had an affair with Cohn, a Jew, at San Sebastián. She then becomes involved with the bullfighter Pedro Romero. Her fiancé Mike Campbell endures all of this. This odd, annoying, yet powerful novel remains a presence in one's mind.

Hemingway had seen *Gatsby* eclipse even *In Our Time* when both appeared in 1925. He has come back now in 1926 with *The Sun Also Rises*, attacking Fitzgerald as Robert Cohn, in a novel that might come close to competing with *Gatsby*, but certainly does not surpass it. He will try again three years later with another great heroine, Catherine Barkley, in another love story, in what might justly be considered the perfection of his style, *A Farewell to Arms*, in 1929.

The rivalry between Fitzgerald and Hemingway could be ugly, although with the ugliness coming entirely from Hemingway. But the rivalry was good for literature if it pushed Hemingway to write his best novel.

CHAPTER FOUR

Hemingway's Best Novel

Hemingway often said that among his novels, *A Farewell to Arms* (1929) was his favorite. It represented a surprising development in his style, more lyrical than anything he had attempted before, moving beyond and enriching what had begun with the vignettes in the 1924 (Paris) *in our time*. There he had been searching for the perfect sentence: "Everybody was drunk. The whole battery was drunk going along the road in the dark." ... "They shot the six cabinet ministers at half-past six in the morning against the wall of a hospital." These vignettes moved forward to become the numbered and italicized "chapters" appearing between the stories in the 1925 *In Our Time*. Yet the more lyrical prose of *A Farewell to Arms* retains the capability, as Edmund Wilson said about that earlier work, of casting a limpid shaft into deep waters. Its opening sentences demonstrate exactly that. In *A Farewell to Arms* Hemingway also achieved for the first time a comprehensive structure by using various motifs, most notably Frederic Henry's spectatorial gaze outward from inside a window, repeated at intervals throughout. Important variations on this motif culminate in the final chapter with two lyrical and elegiac sentences as memorable as the words of any poem.

The opening chapter, in length only a page and a half, begins with that gaze from a window and ends with death and rain: "At the start of the winter came the permanent rain and with the rain came the cholera. But it was checked and in the end only seven thousand died of it in the army." The brief opening chapter anticipates the shape of the novel as a whole, from a gaze out of the window to rain and—associated with rain—death. The narrator Frederic Henry's mention of "only" seven thousand dead suggests ironic understatement as one way of facing catastrophe. In the final sentences of *A Farewell to Arms*, Frederic Henry himself is outside the window and in the rain, while Hemingway's new heroine, Catherine Barkley, a heroine very different from Lady Brett Ashley, lies dead in the hospital.[1]

81

The opening sentences of *A Farewell to Arms* possess the qualities of a good poem. Their cadences imitate the movement of thought, here passive, contemplative. The images have a rare quality, river-plain-mountain sequence representing the movement of the gaze toward the mountains, as the clear and rapidly moving stream attracts the mind and offers a refreshing contrast to the dust to come as its water flows cleanly around the dry and white boulders. It would be a violation to change a single word, and after a few readings the passage becomes part of our minds:

> In the late summer of that year we lived in a house in a village that looked across the river and the plain to the mountains. In the bed of the river there were pebbles and boulders, dry and white in the sun, and the water was clear and swiftly moving and blue in the channels.

Lt. Frederic Henry, telling this story, feels the attraction of those boulders, dry and white, and the clear water. They seem a relief from subjectivity; they are clean, clear, permanent, independent of time and will. In their individual thingness they give him pleasure, reassurance. He wants to linger over each, and they also remain in the reader's mind, as Hemingway's monosyllables slow the pace, the individual words creating a space around each in which suggestion silently trembles and much is left unsaid. One thing unsaid is that Frederic clearly prefers to remain stationary there inside the room; he does not want to join those dusty moving troops outside:

> Troops went by the house and down the road and the dust they raised powdered the leaves of the trees. The trunks of the trees too were dusty and the leaves fell early that year and we saw the troops marching along the road and the dust rising and leaves, stirred by the breeze, falling and the soldiers marching and afterward the road bare and white except for the leaves.

The troops are gone, leaving no address, as it were, and the bare white road remains unchanged by their transitory presence, as if no one had been there at all. The leaves are going, like the soldiers. The repetition of *and* in the unfurling sentence creates a uniform rhythm without subordination, with Frederic Henry passively contemplating the scene. He himself creates the association of leaves-falling-dust-troops. Frederic knows the men are headed up into the mountains, the mountains up where the deadly fighting grinds on. They are headed, like falling leaves, toward death and dust. The suggested but unstated emotion of the sequence of sentences here is fear, a fear more powerful because it is not, cannot, be mentioned. This first chapter reinforces that unstated emotion of fear with multiple other images of infertility and death. On the second page, time passes from "late summer" to fall:

> And in the fall when the rains came the leaves all fell from the chestnut trees and the branches were bare and the trunks black with rain. The vineyards were thin and bare-branched too and all the country wet and brown and dead with the autumn.

Frederic seems entirely disengaged from the war, except for his understated but continuing and willed refusal to be engaged. We hear this mental rhythm again at the beginning of the story "In Another Country" from Hemingway's collection *Men Without Women* (1927): "In the fall the war was always there, but we did not go to it any more." F. Scott Fitzgerald had praised that sentence in a letter to Hemingway (April 18, 1927) as "one of the most beautiful prose sentences I've ever read." This disengagement represents the narrator's "separate peace." Anticipating the shape of the entire novel, the very brief opening chapter establishes a pattern that with repetition and reinforced by other elements creates a powerful sense of inevitability.

Returning to the pattern established in the opening sentences of chapter 1, we find a sequence of other similar but evolving spectatorial gazes by Frederic from a series of other windows. They occur more frequently at the beginning of the novel to establish what might be called the leitmotif of the novel, and then are orchestrated in different modes to explicate themselves. Unaccountably, in all that has been written about *A Farewell to Arms*, this structural element, so carefully wrought by Hemingway, has not, so far as I know, been mentioned. It represents a new capability in his craft as a novelist. At the beginning of chapter 2 we have the first repetition:

> The next year there were many victories. The mountain that was beyond the valley and the hillside where the chestnut forest grew was captured and there were victories beyond the plain on the plateau to the south and we crossed the river in August and lived in a house in Gorizia that had a fountain and many thick shady trees in a walled garden and a wisteria vine purple on the side of the house.

Frederic remains uninvolved here, the first sentence ending with *victories*—ironic, as if they were not really victories, or as if he does not care.

Despite the beauty of some of the painterly details, the lack of subordination in the sentences suggests distance and a kind of weariness. Still in chapter 2, and on the next page:

> Later, below in the town, I watched the snow falling, looking out of the window of the bawdy house, the house for officers, where I sat with a friend and two glasses drinking a bottle of Asti, and, looking out at the snow falling slowly and heavily, we knew it was all over for that year.

The winter passes, spring arrives. Chapter 3 begins with what might be a window view, still a placid and painterly gaze, and with Frederic still safe but with a sinister addition in the words *front* and *guns:*

> When I came back to the front we still lived in that town. There were many more guns in the country around and the spring had come. The fields were green and there were small green shoots on the vines, the trees along the road had small leaves and a breeze came from the sea. I saw the town with the hill and the old castle above it in a cup in the hills with the mountains beyond, brown mountains with a little green on their slopes.

The landscape and the picturesque sights surround and almost absorb the "guns" and the "front" that now apparently are nearby. But at the beginning of chapter 4 the guns begin to climb through the window of the room in which Frederic has been, though apprehensive, "guns" and "front" safe. The chapter begins with menace combined with a touch of comedy:

> The battery in the next garden woke me in the morning and I saw the sun coming through the window and got out of the bed. I went to the window and looked out. The gravel paths were moist and the grass was wet with dew. The battery fired twice and the air came each time like a blow and shook the window and made the front of my pajamas flap. I could not see the guns but they were evidently firing directly over us. It was a nuisance to have them there but it was a comfort that they were no bigger.

That is not an alarm clock waking Frederic, still in his pajamas. And though the garden is there, the war has turned up in it, explosively. The phrase "the battery in the next garden," alarming and amusing, evolves into a certain "comfort," with Frederic relieved to find that the guns "were no bigger." Still, they have reached in and grabbed him by the pajama flap. Detached as he has been, the war is coming after him. Yet we still do not know why he is here. In telling this story he has seemed to avoid that subject, the reason why an American is here on the Italian front, of all places. His explanation, when he gives one later on, is not an explanation at all, and it comes when he has deserted after the Caporetto disaster, having nearly been shot as a deserter by the battle police, and yet managed to escape by diving into the Tagliamento River. Back in Milan he meets an American acquaintance named Simmons who understands that Frederic is "in a jam," and asks him why he has been in Italy. Frederic says only, "I wanted to be an architect." Simmons tactfully lets the matter drop. Obviously, Frederic does not want to discuss the reason. In fact, he never does say, but we can ferret it out, and it is important to *A Farewell to Arms*, though it remains down below the surface of its prose.

The gradually revealing window scenes will evolve and provide more in the pattern they have established. They occur importantly in chapters 1, 2, 3, 4, 5, 6, 10, 16, 34, 36, 38, 39, and, climactically, twice in chapter 40. The second of these, looking out on a garden from Catherine and Frederic's hotel window in Lausanne, constitutes the elegiac, beautiful, and tragic culmination of these window scenes and, though they do not know it, an elegy on what is really their marriage.

In chapter 4, the chapter in which the concussions from big guns have reached into Frederic's comforting bedroom, another major element intrudes: Hemingway's most appealing heroine and, at the end, Frederic's moral exemplar, Catherine Barkley, an English nurse. Taken to meet her by his crony, the cynical and later syphilitic Lieutenant Rinaldi, Frederic first sees her, and—especially in retrospect when we know her fate—the lyrical description possesses understated power:

> The British hospital was a big villa built by Germans before the war. Miss Barkley was in the garden. Another nurse was with her. We saw their white uniforms through the trees and walked toward them.

The white uniforms seen through the trees resemble a nineteenth-century impressionist painting, a Renoir, and the hospital built by Germans before the war reminds us of an older and civilized Europe before this industrialized carnage. Miss Barkley, who will be a heroine of *language,* and the implications of the way she uses it, quickly interrupts some banal small talk:

"*Do* we have to go on and talk this way?"
"No," I said.
"That's a relief. Isn't it?"

Then Frederic asks her about the stick she carries:

> "What is the stick?" I asked. Miss Barkley was quite tall. She
> wore what seemed to me to be a nurse's uniform, was blonde and
> had a tawny skin and gray eyes. I thought she was very beautiful.
> She was carrying a thin rattan stick like a toy riding-crop, bound
> in leather.
> "It belonged to a boy who was killed last year."
> "I'm awfully sorry."
> "He was a very nice boy. He was going to marry me and he was
> killed in the Somme."

Her words *matter,* factual and important, while his are conventional
and banal. A few moments later she remarks: "People can't realize what
France is like. If they did, it couldn't all go on. He didn't have a saber
cut. They blew him all to bits." Immediately, in her directness and truth
telling, she is Frederic's superior, morally and in the verbal style reflecting it, or maybe even creating it as a form of self-discipline. Carrying her
fiancé's swagger stick, Catherine has identified with him, has become a
version of the young officer; she herself uses the language of an officer
under pressure.
    A further comment is in order here regarding Catherine's language.
In *Patria Mia,* written in 1913, Pound noticed "something in the temper
of the [British] race which has strengthened it and given it fibre. And
this is hardly more than a race conviction that words scarcely become a
man." Later, he mentions "the Anglo-Saxon objection to speaking at all."
Catherine Barkley does not waste words, and the worse things get, the
fewer words she uses. The young British officer Catherine had loved and
was going to marry had been killed in those 1916 mass slaughters on the
Somme, thousands dying in a morning "big push," many drowning in the
mud created by rain and earth chewed into mush by the British barrage.
That is why Catherine was "crazy" when she meets Frederic, and why,
through its association with the Somme, rain, and death, she indelibly
fears the rain. At the end of chapter 19 she speaks with Frederic:

> "All right. I'm afraid of the rain because sometimes I see me dead
> in it."

"No."
"And sometimes I see you dead in it."

A moment later:

> "It's all nonsense. It's only nonsense. I'm not afraid of the rain. I'm
> not afraid of the rain. I'm not afraid of the rain. Oh, oh, God, I wish
> I wasn't." She was crying. I comforted her and she stopped crying.
> But outside it kept on raining.

Frederic has been able to interrupt her slide into hysteria, "comforting"
her. Catherine has internalized the death of the young officer in the rain
at the Somme, identifying with him, feeling that they were married, one
person, and now she is beginning to fear for Frederic. He is beginning to
merge for her with the British officer. She has also internalized the authority of an officer, represented by the swagger stick she has inherited. She
begins initiating Frederic into the discipline and realism of such a man.
When they first became acquainted she had rebuked his advances:

> "This is a rotten game we play, isn't it?"
> "What game?"
> "Don't be dull."
> "I'm not, on purpose."
> "You're a nice boy," she said. "And you play it as well as you
> know how. But it's a rotten game."

She wastes no words, tells the truth.

As their relationship develops, it eventually amounts to a marriage if
judged by its seriousness, Frederic soon becoming far from callow and
dull, but still lacking Catherine's wholly achieved discipline, which seems
military, the discipline of an officer. Frederic's famous wound in chapter
9 begins a process of change that is not complete until the last chapter.
Now, however, the wounded Frederic lies prone on a stretcher—a posture
imitating death—in an ambulance on his way to a field hospital. Above
him, also on a stretcher, lies another wounded man who actually bleeds
to death where he lies. Their identical postures associate the two men.
The description of the leaking and then dripping blood tells the story.
"After a while the stream from the stretcher above lessened and started
to drip again and I heard and felt the canvas above move as the man on
the stretcher settled more comfortably." He settles "more comfortably"
because he has died at that moment, a bit of his blood dropping more

slowly on Frederic. Chapter 12 carries forward the image of a prone man, now one on his deathbed:

> If anyone were going to die they put a screen around the bed so you could not see them die, but only the shoes and puttees of doctors and men nurses showed under the bottom of the screen and sometimes at the end there would be whispering.

Frederic Henry is again prone when he sees just what is outside a hospital window, the novel itself since its very first sentences having known what is outside that window:

> When they lifted you up out of bed to carry you into the dressing room you could look out of the window and see the new graves in the garden. A soldier sat outside the door that opened onto the garden making crosses and painting on them the names, rank, and regiment of the men who were buried in the garden.

Death is the realm of fact. That is where many or most of the troops marching up the road to the mountains outside Frederic's window in chapter 1 were headed.

When Frederic has been shipped to the main hospital in Milan, his awareness of death has become sharply personal, and in consequence he is able to experience love for Catherine powerfully and for the first time (chapter 14):

> She came in the room and over to the bed.
> "Hello, darling," she said. She looked fresh and young and very beautiful. I thought I had never seen any one so beautiful.
> "Hello," I said. When I saw her I was in love with her. Everything turned over inside of me. She looked toward the door, saw there was no one, then she sat on the side of the bed and leaned over and kissed me. I pulled her down and kissed her and felt her heart beating.

This is the first time Frederic has seen Catherine since the wound, which has enabled him—because his perceptions have been sharpened by awareness of his mortality—to see Catherine freshly and experience their love with a seriousness created by his experience of death. As John Donne said, "Be absolute for death." Taking a risk we probably do not mind, Hemingway names the benign physician who cares for Frederic "Dr. Valentini." At the beginning of chapter 16 Frederic's hospital room in Milan has become a home with a window view. The "we" of the first sentence of chapter 1, then his army ambulance unit, has been redefined as Catherine and Frederic. They have created a "we" that for a while seems permanent. Their occasional private codelike talk with each other and their private myth of being the same person consolidate their alliance against the war and the world. To use Donne again, they build in their private language "pretty rooms."

> That night a bat flew into the room through the open door that led onto the balcony and through which we watched the night over the roofs of the town. It was dark in our room except for the small light of the night over the town and the bat was not frightened but hunted in the room as though he had been outside. We lay and watched him and I do not think he saw us because we lay so still. After he went out we saw a searchlight come on and watched the beam move across the sky.

The searchlight, looking for bombers, is out there, beyond their window. This idyll, the lovers in the safe room, even the bat not frightened, must in the rhythm of the novel be interrupted. Frederic, recovering, necessarily reports back to his unit at the front; under Austrian pressure the Italian army disintegrates and we have the great account of the chaotic retreat from Caporetto. Frederic executes a deserting sergeant, but the retreat becomes a rout, and Frederic, about to be shot by the battle police, escapes by diving into the Tagliamento River. At length and disguised, he makes his way to a lakeside hotel in Stresa. After the chaos and danger of the retreat, Frederic finds the apparent safety of another "home," and Hemingway writes a beautiful ode to civilization and well-being as Frederic makes his way to the hotel bar where his martini has an almost sacramental character:

> I took a good room. It was very big and light and looked out on the lake. The clouds were down over the lake but it would be beautiful with the sunlight. I was expecting my wife, I said. There was a big double bed, *letto matrimoniale* with a satin coverlet. The hotel was very luxurious. I went down the long halls, down the wide stairs, through the rooms to the bar. I knew the barman and sat on a high stool and ate salted almonds and potato chips. The martini felt cool and clean. . . . The sandwiches came and I ate three and drank a couple more martinis. I had never tasted anything so cool and clean. They made me feel civilized.

Catherine arrives, pregnant, to enhance this civilized "home," and the sense of an older Europe is further suggested by Count Greffi, an ancient billiards expert who actually remembers Metternich. This episode has importance since, at the Congress of Vienna, Metternich led in restoring civilized order to Europe after the Napoleonic Wars. That nineteenth-century Europe is now being shattered by the industrialized modern war.

At the beginning of chapter 36, we have a parallel to that scene from the window in chapter 4, when the impact of the big guns makes Frederic's pajamas flap:

> That night there was a storm and I woke to hear the rain lashing the window-panes. It was coming in the open window. Some one had knocked on the door. I went to the door very softly, not to disturb Catherine, and opened it. The barman stood there. He wore his overcoat and carried his wet hat.

With the rain the barman brings bad news, that the Italian police will arrest Frederic in the morning.

Frederic and Catherine escape across the lake by rowboat to neutral Switzerland, another idyllic home for the winter of 1917 in the alpine hotel run by the Guttingens:

> That fall the snow came very late. We lived in a brown wooden house in the pine trees on the side of the mountain and at night there was frost so that there was thin ice over the water in the two pitchers on the dresser in the morning. Mrs. Guttingen came into the room early in the morning to shut the windows and started a fire in the tall porcelain stove. The pine wood crackled and sparked and then the fire roared in the stove and the second time Mrs. Guttingen came into the room she brought big chunks of wood for the fire and a pitcher of hot water. When the room was warm she brought in breakfast. Sitting up in bed eating breakfast we could see the lake and the mountains across the lake on the French side. There was snow on the tops of the mountains and the lake was a gray steel-blue.

The grasp of detail here accumulates, each delightful detail going to construct their next to last home, in all its reassurance and seeming stability.

Then, with the melting of snow toward the spring, the end comes in Lausanne, where they stay at another fine hotel as Catherine awaits her trip to the hospital. Here we get the final view from the window, an extraordinarily powerful moment since this theme has been so intricately developed:

> The concierge with brass keys on his lapels, the elevator, the carpets on the floors, and the white washbowls with shining fixtures, the brass bed and the big comfortable bedroom all seemed very great luxury after the Guttingens. The windows of the room looked out on a wet garden with a wall topped by an iron fence. Across the street, which sloped steeply, was another hotel with a similar wall and garden. I looked out at the rain falling in the fountain of the garden.

Every detail of that passage deserves examination. Though this room is especially comfortable, there is also a sense of danger. And the details each contribute to a sense of our common fate—the iron fence, the fact that all of the windows look out on the same scene, then the rain falling on the fountain of the garden. Hemingway has worked for those last three sentences since the first sentences of his first chapter. The two lovers are in another of their hotels, the last one for them. Like them, we are all transients, whatever rooms we live in, even if we own a castle. The "other hotels," in a sense identical, universalize what Frederic and Catherine see from this window. The rain is falling in that fountain, here a relative of the Grecian urn, art and death and love, all somehow part of one complex thought that defines the fully human. The fountain, as a work of art, accommodates the rain, in a salute here to art and death.

In his very fine essay "Hemingway and His Critics" (1939), Lionel Trilling writes that Hemingway "has a perfect medium and tells the truth even if it be only *his* truth." This may be correct, but the "only" does not need to be stressed. Hemingway indeed has created the perfect medium, and has at least touched universal truths.

In Catherine Barkley, Hemingway has established a legitimate romantic heroine, the Catherine we remember for example in chapter 23 on the night Frederic must return to the front:

> It was dark outside and cold and misty. I paid for my coffee and grappa and I watched the people going by in the light from the window. I saw Catherine and knocked on the window. She looked, saw me and smiled, and I went out to meet her. She was wearing a dark blue cape and a soft felt hat. We walked along together, along the sidewalk past the wine shops.

Two images of Catherine remain indelibly in the mind, Catherine in her white uniform first seen through the trees, an impressionist painting, and Catherine here as the repeated use of "and" slows the pace, Catherine wearing a dark blue cape and a soft felt hat, a permanent still photograph. Hemingway has a heroine to put against Fitzgerald's debutante Golden Girl, and as we see here this Hemingway heroine comes to us in prose that is in its own way as powerful as Fitzgerald's.

In the last few pages of *A Farewell to Arms,* Catherine, dying during childbirth, again educates Frederic in what she has inherited from the young lieutenant who had been blown to pieces at the Somme, that disciplined and laconic style that is the signature of discipline and courage, and indeed a quality of Hemingway's style before he began to become garrulous during the 1930s. Before that, however, we see that Frederic can still collapse into a self-pitying loss of control, even slide into near hysteria about the possibility that Catherine might die. Fearing for her, he first blames an unknown "they" for her danger:

> Now Catherine would die. That was what you did. You died. You did not know what it was about. You never had time to learn. They threw you in and told you the rules and the first time they caught you off base they killed you. Or they killed you gratuitously like Aymo. Or gave you the syphilis like Rinaldi. But they killed you in the end. You could count on that. Stay around and they would kill you.

Frederic wants to displace agency and depict himself as a victim. But Rinaldi is complicit in his syphilis, Aymo was shot by Italians while trying to flee the rout at Caporetto, and Frederic has had something to do with Catherine's pregnancy. Nor is there some malign god as in Frederic's analogy of the ants and his campfire:

> Once in camp I put a log on top of the fire and it was full of ants. As it commenced to burn, the ants swarmed out and went first toward the centre where the fire was; then turned back and ran toward the end. . . . But I did not do anything but throw a tin cup of water on the log, so that I would have the cup empty to put whiskey in before I added water to it. I think the cup of water on the burning log only steamed the ants.

No, death in this novel has not been caused by some indifferent god, but human beings themselves who inhabit a web of agency. Frederic is not an ant, merely acted upon, but sometimes is an actor. During the rout at Caporetto, he himself has shot the soldier for refusing to obey orders. But all these attempts to distance himself from actuality fail, and his interior monologue shows his language and his emotions whirling out of control:

> Everything was gone inside of me. . . . I knew she was going to die and I prayed that she would not. Don't let her die. Oh, God, please don't let her die. I'll do anything for you if you won't let her die. Please, please, please, dear God, don't let her die.

"Words scarcely become a man," as Pound said in *Patria Mia*. This loss of control violates the ethic of Hemingway's prose. Then, with Frederic at her bedside, it is Catherine who exemplifies the style and control:

> Catherine looked at me and smiled. I bent down over the bed and started to cry.
> "Poor darling," Catherine said very softly. She looked gray.
> "You're all right, Cat," I said. "You're going to be all right."
> "I'm going to die," she said; then waited and said, "I hate it."
> I took her hand . . .
> "Do you want me to get a priest or anyone to come and see you?"
> "Just you," she said. Then a little later, "I'm not afraid. I just hate it."

Moments later:

> "Please go out of the room," the doctor said. "You cannot talk."
> Catherine winked at me, her face gray. "I'll be right outside," I said.
> "Don't worry, darling," Catherine said. "I'm not a bit afraid. It's just a dirty trick."

Catherine winked at me, her face gray. In those moments, the style and the ethic that goes with it pass to Frederic from Catherine, who, herself, had inherited it from the British officer killed at the Somme. We see this in what happens now, as Frederic becomes Catherine's stylistic heir. We also know what the last word of this novel absolutely must be, because as an achieved literary object, *A Farewell to Arms* possesses a perfect shape, the whole making it such a shape by thematic structural elements: "After a while I went out and left the hospital and walked back to the hotel in the rain."

This is not a war novel: The windows of the hotel across the way look out upon an identical garden and the rain falling in the fountain. And all rooms are temporary. Catherine is not killed in the war. Everyone is going to the front. And Catherine Barkley must be one of the great heroines of American or any other literature.

> Outside the room, in the hall, I spoke to the doctor, "Is there anything I can do tonight?"
> "No. There is nothing to do. Can I take you to your hotel?"
> "No, thank you. I am going to stay here a while."
> "I know there is nothing to say. I cannot tell you—"
> "No," I said. "There's nothing to say."
> "Goodnight," he said. "I cannot take you to your hotel?"
> "No, thank you." . . .
> He went down the hall. I went to the door of the room.
> "You can't come in now," one of the nurses said.
> "Yes I can," I said.
> "You can't come in yet."
> "You get out," I said. "The other one too."
> But after I had got them out and shut the door and turned off the light it wasn't any good. It was like saying goodbye to a statue. After a while I went out and left the hospital and walked back to the hotel in the rain.

Hemingway is said to have rewritten that last page fifteen times. He could not get any better than *A Farewell to Arms*. In his style he knew that "words scarcely become a man."

The question now perhaps can be answered. Why did Frederic enlist in the Italian army? And why does he not want to tell anyone his reasons? An answer may come in the following passage in chapter 17, where he reflects on the truth about the war as he is able at this point to put it into words:

> I was always embarrassed by the words sacred, glorious, and sacrifice and the expression in vain. We had heard them, sometimes standing in the rain almost out of earshot, so that only the shouted words came through, and had read them, on proclamations that were slapped up by billposters over other proclamations, now for a long time, and I had seen nothing sacred, and the things that were glorious had no glory and the sacrifices were like the stockyards at Chicago if nothing was done to the meat except to bury it. There were many words that you could not stand to hear and finally only

> the names of places had dignity. Certain numbers were the same
> way and certain dates and these with the names of the places were
> all you could say and have them mean anything.

The noble abstractions had been too distant from the truth and had been
shot out of the language. But the grandest and gravest and most eloquent
abstractions had been those of Woodrow Wilson, "make the world safe
for democracy," "self-determination," all of the famous "fourteen points."
We know from his biographers that the young Ernest Hemingway had
enlisted in the Norton-Harjes Red Cross ambulance unit—virtually a
literary movement—as early as his age permitted, and that he was moti-
vated by such idealism. If Frederic Henry had done the same, then that
might well have accounted for the extreme reaction registered in the quotation about the only things that matter now: those, after all, while valid
as far as they go, are reductive. Why, then, does he tell Simmons he was
in Italy to study architecture? I suppose he thought that he had been a
sucker to believe Woodrow Wilson's nonsense and is embarrassed to say
so. Mark Spilka has suggested that Frederic Henry's name combines that
of Frederic Moreau, the disillusioned hero of Flaubert's *L'éducation senti-
mentale,* with that of Patrick Henry, the idealistic American patriot, which
would explain the peculiar spelling of *Frederic.* But Frederic Moreau,
with his comprehensive disgust, would have been an odd source for the
name of an American child. (So odd a name, in fact, that Hemingway's
biographer Carlos Baker spells it *Frederick.*)

In *A Farewell to Arms* Hemingway perfected his style, the "one perfect
sentence," showing not saying, his style an active element in his showing and integral to the total shape of this novel. Here he combined the
essential style he developed during the early 1920s with a new lyricism
and an enhanced power. It represents an advance over anything he had
done before, and, in his longer forms, something he never achieved again.

After 1929 Hemingway began to slide. As he would have put it, "He
began to slide down and then he slid faster," especially in his first-person
garrulous nonfiction, but with a good recovery in 1936 with "Snows of
Kilimanjaro."[2]

In 1938, with the concentrated two-and-one-half-page story "Old
Man at the Bridge," Hemingway epitomized war in what amounts to an
anecdote from the Spanish Civil War. In 1940, however, he decided to
write a different kind of novel, extensive rather than concentrated, almost
everything apparent on the surface of the narrative. *For Whom the Bell
Tolls* was an enormously popular success, but now seven-eighths of the

iceberg was above the surface of the water, though perhaps Robert Jordan has a hidden impulse toward suicide. Critical reactions were mixed. F. Scott Fitzgerald called it Hemingway's *Rebecca,* referring to the novel by Daphne du Maurier. In his essay "An American in Spain" (1941), Lionel Trilling considered *For Whom the Bell Tolls* to be Hemingway "writing at the top of his bent," a judgment that was certainly wrong.[3] Trilling no doubt was pleased by Hemingway's recovery from *To Have and Have Not* and *The Fifth Column,* both full of posturing and at the time politically correct and artistically negligible popular front attitudes. Trilling commented on a political disconnect. Robert Jordan's disgust with the cynical Stalinists at Gaylord's Hotel and contempt for André Marty, the psychopathic political commissar of the International Brigades who, it was said, kept the firing squads firing, did not, as Trilling put it, "by some failure of mind or of seriousness . . . become integral with the book by entering importantly into the mind of the hero."[4]

A Moveable Feast, published posthumously in 1964, remains of interest as minor Hemingway, containing evocative sketches of Paris and his life with Hadley during the early 1920s when he was beginning to develop the original style that is his central contribution to literature. *A Moveable Feast* is damaged by the malice directed toward the other writers he knew, including the endlessly magnanimous Ezra Pound, and even Gertrude Stein, from whose experiments in prose Hemingway learned a great deal. Yet *A Moveable Feast* exhibits a skill and concision hard to reconcile with the fact that at about the same time he was writing it at the Finca Vigía outside Havana, he was helpless to discipline the metastasizing manuscript of *The Dangerous Summer. Life* had contracted for 10,000 words; Hemingway turned in 120,000, which had to be severely edited. When published as a book in 1985, however, it amounts to good journalism.[5] Valerie Hemingway recalls Hemingway writing *A Moveable Feast* in Cuba:

> Every morning Ernest wrote standing up in his room, carefully pecking out the words on his Royal typewriter. He was finishing the Paris sketches, fine-tuning the chapters he had already written and incorporating his notes. . . . In the spring of 1960 . . . he went over the text carefully a final time, and when he was finished with each chapter, I would retype it.[6]

In *Ernest Hemingway's "A Moveable Feast": The Making of Myth,* Jacqueline Tavernier-Courbin valuably analyzes the evolution and writing of the book, which she regards as a minor masterpiece, but she does not address the discrepancy between the control shown in *A Moveable Feast* and the other posthumously published Hemingway novels.[7] Hemingway's late manuscripts are also verbose and required severe cutting and editing to render them publishable and more or less readable.[8] *The Old Man and the Sea* (1952), a brief parable in mannered cadences, represented a partial comeback. It looks as if Hemingway did in fact write *A Moveable Feast* when it proved impossible for him to discipline the writing of most other works during the later 1950s.

About *A Moveable Feast,* Professor Louis Renza of Dartmouth has advanced the plausible suggestion that in thinking about the early 1920s in Paris, and able to imagine that earlier self writing some five hundred disciplined words a day, Hemingway was able to achieve some of the discipline he had begun to lose after the 1920s.[9] In *A Moveable Feast* we may see Hemingway recovering that early self in the episode "A Good Café on the Place St.-Michel," the expression "*good* place" having a special resonance in Hemingway. Here he recalls writing a story that must have been "The Three-Day Blow" that appeared in *In Our Time* (1925):

> It was a pleasant café, warm and clean and friendly. . . . I took out a notebook from the pocket of the coat and a pencil and started to write. I was writing about up in Michigan and since it was a wild, cold, blowing day it was that sort of day in the story.

In Our Time would be Hemingway's first major book, but that was in the early 1920s, the decade when he produced his best writing.

CHAPTER FIVE

Gilead: A Rumor of Angels

God is the ground of being.
　　　　　—Paul Tillich

"'Everything is full of gods,' exclaimed Thales of Miletus. Biblical mono-theism swept away the gods in the glorification of the majesty of the One, but the fullness that overwhelmed Thales continued to live on for a long time in the figures of the angels, those beings of light, who are witnesses to the divine glory."[1] In the midst of the business of life, "some have entertained the angels unawares" (Hebrews 13:2). In *Gilead* the Reverend John Ames of the small town of Gilead, Iowa, can be said to entertain the angels unawares as a witness to the divine glory. *Gilead* makes central the perception of *Being,* in Heidegger's sense of the term.

Almost anyone would have been struck by James Wood's observation that in Marilynne Robinson's prose in *Gilead,* "silence is itself a quality, and . . . the space around words may be full of noises."[2] James Wood is right about the effect she achieves. And what he saw pulls an immense amount with it, as Joan Acocella recognized in another very fine article.[3]

Gilead brings forward characters who are both memorable and representative of large and difficult ideas made concrete through prose. Marilynne Robinson slows things down much as in an old-fashioned epistolary novel such as *The Sorrows of Young Werther, Clarissa,* or *Julie; or, The New Eloise.* Using a variation of this epistolary form, she allows moments of special experience enough time to live in the mind of the attentive reader. *Gilead* consists entirely of a long letter written by the Reverend John Ames; it does have a plot, but it does not drive the reader urgently ahead. Rather, the letter, while recounting incidents, establishes a meditative pace, inviting you to read patiently, and soon with wonder. Precisely that is the philosophical point of the book: the experience of wonder, of Being. Writing about Proust, Paul Valéry once said that "unconsciously we lend the characters of a novel all the human lives which exist in us potentially." The prose of *Gilead* acts with unusual power to evoke in its reader the capacity for experiencing the moment, to hold the moment steadily in the mind before it loses its immediacy and vanishes into time.

Set in the small and declining Iowa town of Gilead in the year 1956, the narrative consists entirely of a long letter written by the local Congregational minister John Ames, seventy-six, to his son, "not quite seven," by his second and much younger wife. The Reverend Ames has been diagnosed with angina pectoris and knows he will die, probably soon. He wants the boy to read this meditative autobiography in letter form much later, when perhaps he will understand it.

In the town of Gilead out on the bleak prairie, not a great deal happens, except that everything happens. In the three generations of the Ames family we glimpse a decisive part of the history of the United States, including the migration westward, the Civil War, and variations in American Protestantism. And, now, we also glimpse the experience by Ames of what once was known as holiness, and for which the barrenness of the prairie might seem the necessary condition, as he achieves a concentration of mind that enables him to see, to hear, and to reflect on his senses, unusually alive, and through his senses experience the moment in an unusual way: "I have lived my life on the prairie and a line of oak trees can still astonish me." In *Gilead* the individual moment sometimes possesses weight:

> There is a reality in blessing, which I take baptism to be, primarily. It doesn't enhance sacredness, but it acknowledges it, and there is a power in that. I have felt it pass through me, so to speak. The sensation is of really knowing a creature, I mean really feeling its mysterious life and your own mysterious life at the same time.

> There was a young couple strolling along half a block ahead of me. The sun had come up brilliantly after a heavy rain, and the trees were glistening and very wet. On some impulse, plain exuberance, I suppose, the fellow jumped up and caught hold of a branch, and a storm of luminous water came pouring down on the two of them, and they laughed and took off running, the girl sweeping water off her hair and her dress as if she were a little bit disgusted, but she wasn't. It was a beautiful thing to see, like something from a myth. . . .

I was struck by the way light felt that afternoon. I have paid a good deal of attention to light, but no one could begin to do it justice. There was the feeling of a weight of light—pressing the damp out of the grass and pressing the smell of sour old sap out of the boards on the porch floor and burdening the trees a little as a late snow would do. . . .

In those days, as I have said, I might spend most of a night reading. Then, if I woke up still in my armchair, and if the clock said four or five, I'd still think how pleasant it was to walk through the streets in the dark and let myself into the church and watch dawn come in the sanctuary. I loved the sound of the latch lifting. The building has settled into itself so that when you walk down the aisle, you can hear it yielding to the burden of your weight. It's a pleasanter sound than an echo would be, an obliging, accommodating sound. . . . After a while I did begin to wonder if I liked the church better with no people in it

Trees sound different at night, and they smell different, too. . . .

Marilynne Robinson achieves unique effects with her prose. So firm is John Ames's grasp on the world that sometimes every word touches that mysterious life and every word counts: the sound of the latch lifting, the floorboards yielding to his weight. He loves even the "sound of the latch." At moments here nothing is instrumental, a means to some end. Everything is what it is in itself. The state of consciousness sometimes achieved by John Ames lets existence be, experiences it as possessing the philosophical category of Being, the experience of which is the core of Martin Heidegger's philosophy. That verb, Being, a gerund, is going nowhere, is doing nothing beyond itself, but simply and intransitively is. The Reverend John Ames of Gilead, Iowa, meets Saint Anselm of Canterbury, whom apparently he has not read. As existence becomes conscious of itself it reaches its own edges, sees the world with greater and greater clarity, and wonders about its isness. Ames understands the psychological fact that impatience and irritation, so familiar to most of us, are obstacles to seeing the world in this way; indeed they are versions of the sin of anger, one of the seven "deadly" sins, and as such prevent us from seeing the truth of the world as it really is, having a mysterious weight and importance, which leads to the wonder that there is this, rather than nothing at all. In the small town of Gilead, and in the novel Gilead, there is indeed "balm."

The sense of Being achieved by Ames might be compared both in similarity and contrast with the effect created by the edges of Hemingway's prose. *A Farewell to Arms* begins with Lt. Frederic Henry looking out through a window:

> In the late summer of that year we lived in a house in a village that looked across the river and the plain to the mountains. In the bed of the river there were pebbles and boulders, dry and white in the sun, and the water was clear and swiftly moving and blue in the channels.

But the noises surrounding Hemingway's words are not those James Wood heard around the words of John Ames. Through context, there exists immediately an ominous overtone, the threat of non-Being, dread, of imminent nothingness. Immediately after that we read:

> Troops went by the house and down the road and the dust they raised powdered the leaves of the trees. The trunks of the trees too were dusty and the leaves fell early that year and we saw the troops marching along the road and the dust rising and leaves, stirred by the breeze, falling and the soldiers marching and afterward the road bare and white except for the leaves.
>
> The plain was rich with crops; there were many orchards of fruit trees and beyond the plain the mountains were brown and bare. There was fighting in the mountains and at night we could see the flashes from the artillery.

Stillness and motion, life and death, Being and non-Being. There, Frederic Henry, an observer gazing out, does not want to join those marching men, those leaves, that dust. In the silences surrounding Hemingway's words the noises we hear are screams, terror, nothingness, the result of larger prose units than a word itself, the motion of the troops, the dust they raise, soon the "mountains" where the fighting rages and toward which they are marching, to fall as the leaves are falling and become dust themselves like the dust they are raining. Terror is not what surrounds the words of John Ames.

But of course the Reverend John Ames does exist in the flow of time and history. At the beginning of *Gilead* he has a young wife and son. His first wife, a local woman, died in childbirth; their infant daughter, "Angelina," be it noted, also died. Ames then spent his solitary years reading, working nights on his sermons, and by 1956 these sermons amounted to a prodigious number. He calculates the number of words, and so the number of books they would amount to, and in quantity at least he is in the league of Augustine and Calvin. Among modern theologians he is especially close to the neoorthodox Karl Barth. Ames has become a very learned man, steeped in Calvin, his most congenial English authors John Donne and George Herbert, their poems sometimes talking directly to God. We sense this fully absorbed legacy of thought now, as we read his meditative philosophical prose struggling with the concept of Being:

> We participate in Being without remainder. No breath, no thought, no wart or whisker, is not as sunk in Being as it could be. And yet no one can say what Being is. . . . You can assert the existence of something—Being—having not the slightest notion what it is. Then God is at a greater remove altogether.

The Reverend John Ames struggles with this difficult concept and arrives not far from Anselm's *Proslogion;* we can think about a highest form of Being, but then it must exist, since existence trumps idea: therefore God exists. Put nakedly that way, this theory is not very persuasive. But Anselm's argument really rests upon a celebration of existence, which itself is its unstated premise. In Genesis, Yahweh offers, "I Am that I Am." As Paul Tillich put it, "God" is the "ground of being." Martin Heidegger put reflection on Being at the center of his philosophy. He took the simple sentence "I observe that I am," and remarked the "disquiet" that should arise from the "naked that." He wrote of the "curious, astonished, alarmed thinking about the fact that I exist or that anything else exists at all."[4] But relief from such metaphysical anxiety can come from concentration on Being itself, the *isness* of the world. Heidegger found a sense of such moments in Hölderlin and Rilke, poetry and philosophy converging on a fundamental insight.

The emotions of anxiety and dread experienced by Heidegger differ markedly from those of John Ames. Where Heidegger experiences anxiety and dread, Ames experiences wonder, even the presence of the miraculous. This difference very likely is due to the tradition of thought in which Ames locates his experience of Being. One would like to read some of those sermons written out by Ames and stored now in his attic. Marilynne Robinson is rare among modern American novelists in dealing, and being aware of dealing, with important and complex ideas.

In the biblical pattern, Ames's years of loneliness after the death of his first wife constitute his years in the desert, a trial, but also a deepening

experience. Joan Acocella can validly see *Gilead* itself as a journey to salvation like *Pilgrim's Progress*. Ames's erudition provides him with a great
tradition of thought in which to locate his experiences. Indeed, one would
like to read some of those sermons stored in Ames's attic; but alas they
exist only in *Gilead,* or in Marilynne Robinson's mind.

Ames's second marriage comes as a surprise. On a rainy Pentecost Sunday an unfamiliar young woman appears in his church, her eyes sad and
her expression serious. Ames discloses nothing about her past, and may
know nothing about it himself, though he feels that she has had a difficult
life. He surprises himself by immediately falling in love with her, but is
aware of their disparity in ages, she in her thirties, he sixty-six. She continues to appear at his church; she does chores around it, helps him with
his garden. "And one evening when I saw her there, out by the wonderful
roses, I said, 'How can I repay you for this?' And she said, 'You ought
to marry me.' And I did." To Ames we know that existence, the world
itself, is a gift, and this special gift reinforces that perception. The young
woman, there among the roses in the garden, has the quality of Eve at the
beginning of time. Often in Ames's descriptions we have a sense of the
world at the beginning, seen innocently as if seen freshly, as never before.
To this second marriage comes a son for whom he writes in this long letter what it is fair to call his testament.

The first major action described in *Gilead* consists of an arduous journey
in which Ames's father, also named John Ames, takes him on a search for
his grandfather's grave. The trip brings hunger, thirst, and sometimes danger; they are even shot at, and the landscape they cross is usually bleak.
This pilgrimage with his father to a desolate Kansas grave constitutes a
preface to the larger pilgrimage of John Ames, which becomes the subject
of the entire novel. Along their trek to Kansas, Ames's father tells him a
good deal about his grandfather. The grave when they reach it amounts
to very little, overgrown with weeds, with the name, John Ames, spelled
by nails hammered into a log and bent:

> That graveyard was about the loneliest place you could imagine. . . .
> It was hard to imagine the grass had ever been green. Everywhere you
> stepped, little grasshoppers would fly up by the score, making that
> snap they do, like striking a match. My father put his hands in his
> pockets and looked around and shook his head. Then he started cut-
> ting the brush back with a hand scythe he had brought, and we set up
> the markers that had fallen over—most of the graves were just out-
> lined with stones, with no names or dates or anything on them at all.

In this wasteland they do what they can to remember and honor the dead and bring to his grave a decent order; and then, as if a result, young Ames witnesses a spectacle that remains with him as a vision—while the sun goes down in the west, a full moon rises in the east:

> At first I thought I saw the sun setting in the east; I knew where east was, because the sun was just over the horizon when we got there that morning. Then I realized that what I saw was a full moon rising just as the sun was going down. Each of them was standing on its edge, with the most wonderful light between them. It seemed as if you could touch it, as if there were palpable currents of light passing back and forth, or as if there were great taut skeins of light suspended between them. . . . We just stood there until the sun was down and the moon was up.

In his poem "Correspondences," Baudelaire said that nature is a forest of symbols observing our passage with accustomed eyes; this may be a symbol of death and resurrection, even a complex and not altogether favorable comment on Ames's grandfather's Old Testament fanaticism in the cause of abolition. As the reader proceeds in the narrative, the novel *Gilead* itself acquires the character of a quest, the Reverend John Ames moving among dangers and temptations, one of them the Cromwellian fury of the grandfather's fight against slavery.

The old man had been born in Maine, young Ames's father tells him while on their journey to Kansas. At the age of fifteen he had a vision of Jesus in chains, his wrists in manacles that cut to the bone. Thus commanded to fight in the antislavery cause, he headed west during the 1830s, following the trail of many New Englanders. In Kansas his church became a stable and outpost for John Brown's night riders, the grandfather joining them. In "bleeding Kansas," as it was called, a preliminary civil war was going on as Brown's men and proslavery Kansans battled over the direction of the state, free soil or slave state. John Ames's father tells the boy of being "awakened by sounds in the night and of walking outside and seeing old John Brown's mule coming out through the doors of his father's church. . . . The church smelled like horses and gunpowder."

One night, the grandfather accosted a soldier following them, shooting him and letting him die in the road. His sermon the following Sunday reeked of blood. With his gun in his belt he preached the young men to war, as young Ames remembers being told:

"It was the very next Sunday the old devil preached in one of those shirts, with that gun in his belt. And you would not have believed how the people responded, all the weeping there was and the shouting." And after that, he said, his father would be gone for days sometimes. There were Sundays when he would ride his horse right up to the church steps just when it was time for service to begin and fire that gun in the air to let the people know he was back. They'd find him standing in the pulpit, with his eyes red and his face pale and dust in his beard, all ready to preach on judgment and grace. My father said, "I never dared to ask him what he'd been up to. I couldn't risk the possibility of knowing things that were worse than my suspicions."

Too old to be a combat soldier, the grandfather served as a chaplain, but fought anyway and lost an eye. Ames's father fought too, but the experience made him a pacifist. Ames remembers the grandfather as he was when he retired to Gilead and lived with the family when Ames was twelve. His recollections of the old man are at once impressive and comic: "My grandfather seemed to me stricken and afflicted, and indeed he was, like a man everlastingly struck by lightning, so that there was an ashiness about his clothes and his hair never settled and his eye had a look of tragic alarm when he wasn't actually sleeping." He was "a wild-haired, one-eyed, scrawny old fellow with a crooked beard like a paintbrush left to dry with lacquer on it." When his one eye looked at the boy it was "like being poked with an accusatory stick." Once when young Ames entered the house, his mother told him that "the Lord is in the parlor." The boy looked in and saw the old man talking with Jesus, "attentive and sociable. . . . I would hear a remark from time to time, 'I see your point,' or 'I have often felt that way myself.' "

But Ames's father breaks with the old man's version of Christianity, asserting the claims of peace:

My father stood up from his chair. He said, "I remember when you walked to the pulpit in that shot-up, bloody shirt with that pistol in your belt. And I had a thought as powerful and clear as any revelation. And it was, This has nothing to do with Jesus. Nothing. Nothing. And I was, and I am, as certain of that as anyone could ever be of any so-called vision. I defer to no one in this. Not to you, not to Paul the Apostle, not to John the Divine. Reverend."

It is possible for zeal, a form of anger, to stand between the mind and Being, that is, between the mind and the perfection of Being, or God.

But if bellicose fanaticism is a temptation, we might reflect at this point that its opposite extreme, pacifism, may be a temptation as well. Was Jesus a pacifist? In the Gospels the evidence on that point is scanty, but we might examine the parable of the Good Samaritan. Suppose the man from Samaria had come along earlier, when the thieves were assaulting and robbing that man on the Jericho road, apparently a dangerous place. The goodness of the Samaritan might well have required that he draw his sword. Ames's father, in his pacifism, has gone to the other extreme from the grandfather. After the quarrel over the meaning of Jesus, the grandfather returns to Kansas, where he now lies in the ground where the Civil War might be said to have begun with John Brown. Ames wonders whether he is the lesser man as measured against his father and grandfather, but his sense of the world as a gift, as Being, is a deeper thing than their quarrel. John Ames now represents a transcending third possibility, neither bellicosity nor pacifism. If we attend to the teaching of the Sermon on the Mount, what we come out with is the state of mind implicitly urged for the Good Samaritan. Yes, he might have to battle the thieves on that dangerous road, perhaps kill them, but he is not to feel anger, rage, bloodlust, as might a warrior such as Achilles; rather, he should feel deep sorrow over the distorted souls of the thieves. The rage of Achilles distorts the soul. Young Ames resolves the grandfather-father dialectic, concluding about his father,

> I loved him with the strangest, most miserable passion when he stood there preaching about how the Lord hates falsehood and how in the end all our works will be exposed in the naked light of truth.

That belief, arising out of Ames's experience and transcending the quarrel between his father and grandfather, gives him the strength to resist the challenge of one form of modernity exemplified by Ludwig Feuerbach. Ames's older brother, Edward, thought to be the brighter of the two, has been the beneficiary of a collection taken up by the parishioners and gone to Göttingen for postgraduate work. He returns a brilliant young man, a cosmopolitan atheist with a mustache and a walking stick, and precipitates a crisis with Ames's father by refusing to say grace at dinner. He also gives young Ames a copy of Feuerbach's *The Essence of Christianity*. Completely unshaken by Feuerbach's negations, he recalls,

> Feuerbach is a famous atheist, but he is about as good on the joyful aspects of religion as anybody, and he loves the world. Of course he thinks religion could just stand out of the way and let joy exist pure

and undisguised. That is his one error, and it is significant. But he is
marvelous on the subject of joy, and also on its religious expressions.

Here, it is credible that Ames was untouched by Feuerbach's negations.
His sensibility would have resisted them with his own experience of
Being, which is the basis of everything. But as the seventy-six-year-old
Ames writes to his son, his formulation—"That is his one error, and it is
significant"—comes from the learned man who is deeply read in theology.
Certainly Edward's refusal to say grace, and so making a scene at dinner, was atrocious. The family dinner table is not the place for disruptive
pride. Ames's own confidence is shown when he tells his almost seven-
year-old son that he has made some notes in that copy of Feuerbach that
he might find useful. He hopes with some confidence that his young son,
who by then will have read and understood this long letter, will have
been immunized against what Feuerbach represents, and thinking now of
Edward as he looked when he returned from Göttingen, he says,

> I'm not saying never doubt or question. The Lord gave you a mind
> so that you would make honest use of it. I'm saying you must be
> sure that the doubts and questions are your own, not, so to speak,
> the mustache and walking stick that happen to be the fashion of
> any particular moment.

Well along in the narrative the energy generated by the grandfather is
replaced by another kind of energy, now far along toward pure negation.
This challenges Ames far more than Feuerbach's atheism ever could. A
cold wind blows in, and those passages expressing a luminous sense of
Being grow much less prominent in the narrative. A new character enters,
bringing something completely discordant, a remarkable invention, and
a problem for everyone in the novel. Not since Thomas Mann's Mynheer
Peeperkorn in *The Magic Mountain* have I seen a narrative shift and reen-
ergize this way, even constituting a fresh theological challenge for Ames.
It will require all his erudition and courage to meet it.
   During his years of loneliness after the death of his first wife, Louisa,
and her infant daughter, a child is born to the wife of the Presbyterian
minister in Gilead, the Reverend Boughton, who was Ames's boyhood
friend and still remains his closest one. This child turns out to be anything
but a blessed event. Aware of Ames's loneliness, the Reverend Boughton
asked Ames to baptize the child. During the ceremony, Boughton surprises him by declaring his name to be John Ames Boughton, no doubt
intending this as an honor. As a boy, "Jack" begins a career of destruction

beginning with pranks that in their originality signal something more than whims, sometimes even a negative exertion of mind. When a list of some of these is made, they amount to a negative counterpart of the quotations listed earlier from Ames that serially form perceptions of the Being of the world, its beauty, and his sense of it as a gift.

> I was thinking about the time when he was just ten or twelve and he filled my mailbox with wood shavings and set them on fire. He rigged up a sort of fuse of twine dipped in paraffin. At that time the mailbox was on a post by the gate. It was that loaf-shaped kind people use in the country. I was walking home from the church in the dark of a winter evening. I heard a poof and looked up, and just then flames came pouring out of the mouth of that box. It gave me quite a turn. But I didn't doubt for a minute whose prank it was. . . .

> I remember coming out of the house one morning and finding my front steps painted with molasses. The ants were so thick they were piling over each other. They were just absolutely solid. Now, you have to ask yourself, How lonely would a child have to be to have time to make such a nuisance of himself? He developed some method for breaking my study windows so that the whole pane would shatter altogether. It was remarkable. I will ask him how he did that, someday when our souls are at peace and we can laugh about it. . . . Once, he took that old Greek Testament right off my desk. If ever there was a thing on earth so little worth the trouble of stealing I don't know what it would be. Once, he stole my reading glasses . . . [then] a little photograph in a velvet case of Louisa, taken when she was a child. I was as angry about that as I have ever been in my life. Just the sheer meanness of it. And how could I tell Boughton that he had done such a thing? How could I say the words? . . .

> That is the sort of thing he did as a young boy, mischief only bordering on harm, generally speaking. That is my belief, though certain harmful things . . . Certain harmful things were done which I have never wished to ascribe to him but which, in the privacy of my thoughts I always did. For example, there was a barn fire, and some animals were lost in it. I may be wrong in blaming him for that.

But the reader by this time blames him. One caper seems right out of a tall tale by Mark Twain. Jack steals a Model T in downtown Gilead, drives it out into the country until it runs out of gas, and then just walks home. Some young fellows with a team of horses pull it to the nearby town of Wilkinsburg and trade it for a hunting rifle, and then it is traded from one person to another as people realize it is stolen and are unwilling to keep it. In effect, Jack criminalizes the whole area: "It was Jack himself who told me he had done it. He'd kept the handle from the glove box as a souvenir and he showed it to me, but I would have believed him anyway."

> Then he started doing the things that got his name in the news-paper, stealing liquor and joyriding, and so on. I've known young fellows who spent time in jail or got themselves sent off to the navy for behavior that wasn't any worse. But his family was so well respected that he . . . was allowed to go right on disgracing his family.

Jack's destructiveness increases during his college years, when, equipped with a Plymouth convertible and his varsity letter sweater, he locates a young, ignorant, and very poor woman who lives in a rural hovel. She becomes pregnant with Jack's child. Though he never acknowledges the baby girl, the Boughton family tries to contribute to her support until her early death through an infection. Jack disappears from Gilead for many years, returning in his forties when his father is elderly, partly crippled, and evidently does not have long to live. This brings the narrative up to the present, in 1956. Ames instinctively fears for his own wife and child:

> Having looked over these thoughts I set down last night, I realize I have evaded what is for me the central question. That is: How should I deal with these fears I have, that Jack Boughton will do you and your mother harm, just because he can, just for the sly, unanswerable meanness of it . . . if he harmed you in the slightest way, I'm afraid theology would fail me.

Ames is in the strange position of having baptized this child and bestowed his own name on him, becoming in that sense his father, but now fearing him.

There transpires an extraordinary scene in which Jack does attempt exactly the sort of invasion and damage Ames fears. One evening after dinner, while Ames and his wife are sitting on the porch, Jack stops by and, while Ames pretends to doze off, begins a conversation that has disturbing overtones. Ames's wife refuses when Jack tries to get her to complain about the confined life she leads in Gilead. They speak of loneliness, which led both to walk the streets and look with longing into people's windows—whether Jack, one senses, has done so or not. A certain closeness seems to be established through their shared memories of loneliness. She mentions that she has had a troubled past, the first time we have heard this, and we wonder if she has told the complete story to Ames:

> There was a silence, and then she said, "You'll be going back to St. Louis?"
>
> *"That's possible."* [italics added]
>
> Another silence. He struck a match. I could smell the smoke of a cigarette.
>
> "Would you care for one?"
>
> "No, thank you." She laughed. "Sure I would. It just isn't seemly in a preacher's wife."
>
> "'It just isn't seemly.' I guess they've been after you."
>
> "I don't mind," she said. "Somebody had to tell me a few things sooner or later. Now I've been seemly so long I'm almost beginning to like it."

Some sort of precipice seems near at hand. Jack's "that's possible," about returning to St. Louis, may be sinister. What would it take to keep him in Gilead? But Ames tells us that "she found my hand and took it between her two warm hands. . . . I was about to show some signs of stirring, just to extricate myself from this discreditable situation I had put myself into, which seemed almost to be spying." In fact, it was spying, and only Jack could have drawn him into this "discreditable situation," of course fearing Jack but also probably not entirely confident of his young wife. Jack soon returns to the theme of his own loneliness: he was planning to walk the streets, looking into windows, imagining what it was like not to be lonely. After a silence she says, "Well, Jack, bless your heart." He replies, "Why, I thank you for that, Lila." This is the first time we have heard the young wife's name, and especially because it is Jack who utters it, the sound of her name comes as a shock, a violation. But her "Well, Jack, bless your heart" is at once a sign of understanding and also a rebuff. Whatever Jack's explorations might have had in mind, certainly not a blessing, this moment will lead to nothing further. The scene, however, leaves a remarkable impression of evil. A cold gale has blown, but the Ames household stands.

From time to time in the past, Jack, seeking out Ames as a clergyman, has had apparently serious talks with him, notably about the doctrine of predestination:

> I was sitting there listening to old Boughton ramble along (he uses
> the expression himself) . . . when Jack broke in and said to me, "So,
> Reverend, I would like to hear your views on . . . predestination."
>   Now, that is probably my least favorite topic of conversation
> in the entire world. I have spent a great part of my life hearing
> that doctrine talked up and down, and no one's understanding ever
> advanced one iota.

Jack presses him. Both Ames and the reader suspect that Jack is merely
playing with him. Or is Jack tormented by self-knowledge concerning the
direction he has been taking? He presses Ames about what the clergyman
tells other people about predestination, and Ames replies,

> "I tell them there are certain attributes our faith assigns to God:
> omniscience, omnipotence, justice, and grace. We human beings
> have such a slight acquaintance with power and knowledge, so little
> conception of justice, and so slight a capacity for grace, that the
> workings of these great attributes together is a mystery we cannot
> hope to penetrate."
>   *He laughed.* [italics added]

That, very likely, has been the goal of Jack's questions from the beginning. Ames has outlined attributes of God about which we can imagine
some slight knowledge, but of how they cohere ultimately in the mind of
God we are helpless to know.[5] He has done well, but Jack's goal seems
to have been to make a fool of him, and Jack must think he has done so
as he laughs. He pushes Ames further, and ends with an insult by calling
him *cagey,* a word entirely inappropriate to the difficulties of Calvin's
theology. Jack is Ames's namesake and godchild, and a conversation like
this stands as a contrast to the instruction Ames gives to the boy who
will read this letter. The reader might well long to deal harshly with Jack,
metaphorically grinding underfoot this insinuating viper. There is a point
at which malice is beyond verbal correction.

But somehow crushing Jack now would already be too late for yet another
family. In the final section of the book, Jack's life while away in St. Louis
is brought into the narrative, and there his destructive capability appears
with even greater effect. The final section of the novel opens with,

> Jack Boughton has a wife and a child. He showed me a picture of
> them. He only let me see it for half a minute, and then he took it

back. I was slightly at a loss, which he must have expected, and still I could tell it was an effort for him not to take offense. You see, the wife is a colored woman. That did surprise me.

This brings forward the theme of race relations begun with Ames's abolitionist warrior-preacher grandfather. Jack's marriage—his wife's name is Della—has never been formalized, but, he chillingly says, it is "a marriage in the eyes of God." The marriage immediately runs into trouble. Jack's black in-laws in Memphis will not accept him, and her father, a minister, though admiring the abolitionist grandfather, contradictorily says that all white men are atheists. Back in St. Louis, Jack and Della are seen together in a park and he loses his job. Then, unable to earn enough to support his family, he sees that his marriage is doomed. We last see Jack when he returns briefly to Gilead, his father now a fragile old man and probably to die soon, in his suffering saying that "Jesus never had to be old." When Jack announces that he will leave Gilead despite his father's deathbed condition, his mother says, "This is it. This is your masterpiece." She knows Jack.

What are we to make of this race-related disaster? The year is 1956. The civil rights revolution is in its early stages. But *Gilead* appeared in 2004. We could say merely that this is how the marriage would end, given what we know of Jack Boughton. Or, fifty years after the beginnings of the civil rights movement, it could represent Marilynne Robinson's judgment that it is very far from achieving the goals of the old Reverend John Ames, the abolitionist grandfather. In her politics, Marilynne Robinson is a Christian morally committed to equality and inclusiveness for American blacks. In her collection of essays *The Death of Adam* (1998), she also criticizes energetically those Christians who neglect Christian teachings about the poor, and she is a strong advocate of conservation, as may be inferred from the role of landscape in *Gilead*. It ends with John Ames reaffirming Being as he contemplates the prairie. He has won through, weathered the storm.

With Jack Boughton out of Gilead, as Joan Acocella says, calm can return.[6] Jack is gratuitously destructive and has been destructive, even ingeniously destructive, since a boy. It would be technically incorrect to say that he is evil, for if he were, evil being non-Being, he could not exist. Still, Jack, short of murder, strews non-Being wherever he goes. Ames has been engaged in a metaphysical agon with Jack, his own spirit roiled by the conflict, and so, as *Gilead* comes to its end, the sense of Being that characterized his narrative before Jack now returns. Ames knows the spiritual price he has paid in the struggle. Taking leave of Jack, he says, "I understand why you have to leave, I really do." Then he reflects, "That was as true a thing as I have ever said. And I will tell you, remarkable as it seemed to me, at that moment I felt grateful for all my old bitterness of heart." That indeed is remarkable insight: he is grateful for the bitterness because of the joy he feels in his recovery. Ames is the spiritually wounded veteran of the spiritual struggle, but Being has triumphed over non-Being and so he can bless Jack as he leaves Gilead, forever.

The phrase from Jeremiah "balm in Gilead" refers to an ancient city east of the Jordan River that evidently dispensed a healing medicament. It possesses a heroic tradition as the place where Ahab, king of Israel, died in battle against the Arameans. All of these associations possess connections with the town of Gilead in the novel.

At the end of the novel, Ames, having battled negation and non-Being, has returned to himself:

> It has seemed to me sometimes as though the Lord breathes on this poor gray ember of Creation and it turns to radiance—for a moment or a year or the span of a life. And then it sinks back into itself again, and to look at it no one would know it had anything to do with fire, or light. That is what I said in the Pentecost sermon. I have reflected on that sermon, and there is some truth in it. But the Lord is more constant and far more extravagant than it seems to imply. Wherever you turn your eyes the world can shine like transfiguration. You don't have to bring a thing to it except a little willingness to see. Only, who could have the courage to see it?

At the outset, the journey by Ames and his father to the grandfather's grave in Kansas has been both an ordeal and a pilgrimage. So is the entire narrative of *Gilead,* challenges including the ordeal imposed by Jack that Ames survives this way:

> I love the prairie! So often I have seen the dawn come and the light flood over the land and everything turn radiant at once, that word "good" so profoundly affirmed in my soul that I am amazed that I should be allowed to witness such a thing. There may have been a more wonderful first moment "when the morning stars sang together and all the sons of God shouted for joy," but for all I know to the contrary, they still do sing and shout, and they certainly might well. Here on the prairie there is nothing to distract attention from the evening and the morning, nothing on the horizon to abbreviate or to delay. Mountains would seem an impertinence from that point of view. . . . I love this town. I think sometimes of going into the

> ground here as a last wild gesture of love—I too will smolder away
> the time until the great and general incandescence.
>
> I'll pray that you grow up a brave man in a brave country. I will
> pray you find a way to be useful.
>
> I'll pray, and then I'll sleep.

During the winter of 2005–2006, New Yorkers had the opportunity to visit an exhibition of great paintings at the Metropolitan Museum. The Renaissance master by the name of Guido de Pietro (1395–1455) had the ability to bring "celestial essences down to earth, gently," wrote art historian Peter Schjeldahl. "Just think of Heaven, he implies, and its soaring immateriality will suffuse the here and now, making a miracle of physical existence."[7] Rev. John Ames, meet the painter known as Fra Angelico.

In Marilynne Robinson we have an American novelist possessing large and important ideas along with the ability to embody them in fiction, an unusual and a welcome phenomenon in the contemporary novel.

CHAPTER SIX

Mann's *Doctor Faustus:*
The Moment in the Depths of Silence

Accurate scholarship can
Unearth the whole offence
From Luther until now
That has driven a culture mad.
                    —W. H. Auden, "September 1, 1939"

Be still, and know that I am God.
                    —Psalm 46:10

Though Marilynne Robinson's *Gilead* appeared in 2004 and Mann's *Doctor Faustus* in 1947, *Doctor Faustus* concludes this study because of its cultural weight and summarizing sweep. Indeed, it can serve as a summary of much that has gone before in this book. Adding to the cultural weight here, Mann accomplishes something unusual, even unique: with his modernist composer Adrian Leverkühn he produced a credible portrait of a genius, a rarity in literature. Perhaps as credible geniuses we can include Socrates and Jesus, who wrote nothing, so the accounts we have of them might be considered literature. But that shows how rare Mann's achievement actually is.

Gilead brought forward Heidegger's perception of Being as a profound experience, indeed a kind of transcendence. Like other modernist works, *Doctor Faustus* reaches the goal of establishing a moment beyond the flux of time, its vehicle modernist music, but with philosophical implications. Mann's *Faustus* reaches back through Goethe's *Faust* to Marlowe's *Tragical History of Doctor Faustus*. Mann's *Doctor Faustus* is a modernist novel about modernism, its Faustian hero Adrian Leverkühn resembling Arnold Schoenberg and his revolutionary twelve-tone scale. The devil appears in this novel, as he does in *The Brothers Karamazov,* and while we may think the devil an illusion here, a sequence of strange and chilling events suggests otherwise.

At the beginning of chapter 2 the narrator introduces himself. "My name is Serenus Zeitblom, Ph.D. . . . My age is sixty, for I was born A.D. 1883, the eldest of four brothers and sisters, at Kaisersaschern. . . . In the same town it was that Leverkühn too spent his school-days." This slightly pompous introduction, with its sense of normality, contrasts in a comic way with the astonishing events in the story he tells.

Doctor Faustus possesses an extensive historical sweep, going back to Luther and moving forward to the end of the Second World War. It addresses a subject central to our time in Germany, the once civilized heart of Europe, where an astonishing nihilism appeared that amounted to a black hole in Western civilization. In *Doctor Faustus* the great German humanist Thomas Mann confronted this negation. The narrative time of *Doctor Faustus* embraces the modern history of Germany, ending with the 1945 total defeat and the opening of the death camps, themselves a demonic nihilism. That military disaster has a Faustian character, but Mann's Faust, the modernist composer Adrian Leverkühn—while pushing his music to its furthest margin, to the truth in the depths of silence—is a *redemptive* Faust. This was the twentieth century, and though Marlowe's Faustus could see "Christ's blood streaming in the firmament," that was beyond Mann. But in his last composition, *The Lament of Doctor Faustus,* he expresses a "hope beyond hope" through the echo in the mind of a high G on a cello that remains for a moment before fading away. This is another example of the special moment that points toward a redemption beyond time and space. In a more mundane way, Leverkühn himself was redemptive for an individual. This occurs in a remarkable love story that takes place in an old-fashioned story-within-the-story.

It is time to reengage critically with the achievement of Thomas Mann. While the works of Joyce and Proust remain firmly in the canon as modernist classics, Mann, after the middle of the twentieth century, tended to recede from our discussion. A good place to begin a reassessment would be *Doctor Faustus*—itself not especially well received, though I judge it a masterpiece—which represents Mann's farewell and indeed can be regarded as a *summa.* The case for *Doctor Faustus* can be made by a careful consideration of structure, theme, and detail. With a Faustian tragic hero, it is a Faustian work itself. Obeying the imperative to "make it new," the modernist composer Adrian Leverkühn presses against the existing frontiers of music and strives heroically to transcend them. For this he seeks a special and deadly stimulus, deliberately infecting himself with syphilis. *Doctor Faustus,* considered as a novel—using as it does a symphonic organization of interwoven themes, and with its lengthy and expert descriptions of music, including Leverkühn's revolutionary advances—also presses hard against and goes beyond the established form of the novel. As it describes music at inspired length, the novel itself seems to be trying to become music. In that, Mann resembles other great modernists, Joyce pressing the frontiers of language and going beyond *Ulysses* to *Finnegans Wake,* and Proust, writing at an unprecedented length unlikely ever to be attempted again. As in these novels, and in Leverkühn's music, modernism often consists of extremes managed by genius. The Renaissance Faust legend originated in the 1587 German chapbook *Historia von D. Johann Fausten,* based on the life of an actual necromancer who died about 1540. In English, Christopher Marlowe drew on the legend for his *Tragical History of Doctor Faustus* (1604), and Shakespeare might be said to have answered Marlowe with *The Tempest* (1611). Where Marlowe's Faustus at the end says, "I'll burn my books" (the fate of heretics), Prospero, a benevolent necromancer, and with all the difference between fire and water, says, "I'll drown my books." *The Tempest,* its text noticeably short for a five-act Shakespearean drama, is a play full of songs, dance, and instrumental music that tends to transcend drama and become music; as a whole, it almost takes the form of a masque. *The Tempest* is a celebration of forgiveness, marriage, and harmony, that is to say, salvation, its music the expression of that harmony. Mann sees his *Doctor Faustus* as expressing the end of Christian humanist optimism as represented by *The Tempest,* and ends *Doctor Faustus* with the consuming fire of the Third Reich in 1945.

In the ambition of *Doctor Faustus,* Mann himself, as I have said, was Faustian; his wife Katia and his daughter Erika affectionately called him *der Zauberer* (the wizard), and indeed he saw himself as possessing a form of forbidden knowledge—the alienation of the artist as represented in part by his homoeroticism, and his rejection of the bourgeois and the normal. Throughout his life Mann was strongly attracted to young men, but there is no doubt that he loved his wife and saw himself as a responsible paterfamilias, always dressed with impeccable formality, the dubiously respectable artist turbulent within.

In 1955, Marguerite Yourcenar judged that

> the works of Thomas Mann have attained to that rare category, the
> modern classic . . . worthy of being taken up again and again for
> examination and reconsideration in all their aspects and at every

level of their meaning; they serve to nourish the mind, but to test it as well. Such works appeal to us on a fourth or fifth reading for reasons quite different from what made us like them in the first place, or even for opposite reasons.[1]

For Thomas Mann, in Yourcenar's first sentence one might have substituted Proust or Joyce as acknowledged modern classics. Such has long been my experience in reading Thomas Mann. Indeed, Yourcenar expressed a consensus in 1955. But not long after that Mann's critical standing was revised downward. His claim to greatness and especially his semiofficial standing as a "spokesman" for humanism and civilization became an annoyance. Most objectionable perhaps was his belief in the capacity of ideas to address a contemporary circumstance that seemed beyond rationality: absurd. Thus F. W. Dupee, an exceptionally sensitive cultural barometer, writing soon after Yourcenar, could describe Mann as a classic that seems "too surgically expert and complacently omniscient."[2] By "omniscient" Dupee meant Mann's implicit claim that such a work as *Doctor Faustus* can comment valuably on the Nazi death factories, or the Gulag, or the bomb. From that perspective, the grandness of Mann's ambition was unwelcome, even foolish. Our reality is too large, too overwhelming, for contemplation other than in nervous fragments, dark ironies, or witty disengagement. To be sure, *Doctor Faustus* does not "explain" Auschwitz, and in fact sees the death factories as a black hole or moral antimatter in Western history; yet *Doctor Faustus* does in fact engage Auschwitz, and despite such terrible knowledge *does* affirm the value of contemplating that history as expressed in the great positive creation that this, and all great works of mind and art, represents. It may even be, *Doctor Faustus* implies, that if we *know enough,* we will not be taken unawares when evil returns in yet another drastic and incommensurate form. To open *Doctor Faustus* again is to open a late modernist work, a novel under radical strain that seeks by an effort of mind to give shape to a world of extreme experience, and by doing so to exert a form of control over it. This in itself is bracing. "The artist always carries a work of art as a whole within himself," observed Mann. "Although aesthetics may insist that musical and literary works, in contradistinction to the plastic arts, are dependent on time and succession of events, it is also true that even such works strive at every moment to be present as a whole."[3] After several readings, and despite its intimidating complexity, Mann's *Doctor Faustus* does achieve actuality as a work that strives toward a shape, though a complex one, a shape that is indeed present as a whole in the mind of the attentive reader. It can have the effect of being written by a God who, having immersed himself in Calvin's *Institutes,* had designed *Doctor Faustus* and set the whole complex mechanism in motion. Yet the novel is more surprising than that suggests, and *Doctor Faustus* demands its own pace in reading, slowly and carefully, and asks repeated rereading before it fully establishes itself, each detail in place, each exactly where it must be.

To experience this large shape emerging constitutes one of its many intellectual pleasures, as does the ultimate shape this novel makes in the mind. Along with its structured quality it includes a number of surprising "grace notes" that provide unanticipated pleasures, including one of the strangest of love stories. And overall Mann deploys extraordinary erudition, much of which the reader must excavate, which, always interesting in itself, also becomes integral to the whole. It is as if the book says aloud to the reader, "You have wondered about Western civilization? Well, here it is. Value it, and defend it." At its core, *Doctor Faustus* does make a major statement about its own era, the terrible first half of the twentieth century with its two European convulsions, millions dying, cities burned to ashes, and the very bases of civilization spectacularly assaulted. No wonder the major late piece of music written by Mann's hero, the composer Adrian Leverkühn, is a work of last days, an apocalypse in the form of an oratorio.

Doctor Faustus sets up correspondences among the three artists Thomas Mann, Adrian Leverkühn, and, yes, Adolf Hitler, each of them a modernist artist in his way, Hitler's art unfortunately not music, painting, or literature, but highly effective political oratory.

In Adrian Leverkühn (*lever:* life, vitality; *kühn:* boldness, danger), *Doctor Faustus* brings us the only credible genius in literature since Prince Hamlet. Such a project, because the figure at its center is unique, tends to require a trustworthy, ordinary sort of narrator, here the intellectually mediocre humanist, Adrian's friend since their childhood, Serenus Zeitblom, the serene flower of time, the culturally impoverished heir of Renaissance humanism. We know that Zeitblom could not have invented the startling Leverkühn. As reliable witnesses, the four narrators of the Gospels perform the same function: they could not have invented, and do not come close to possessing themselves, such language as Jesus uses. Their narrative prose is workmanlike. Highly precocious, Jesus disputes with the rabbis at the temple, scholars judge at about the age of twelve. Later, with almost every remark he makes, the young man from Nazareth adds something permanent to the language.

An ordinary man at the outset, Serenus Zeitblom changes as the narration goes forward, until his total experience, not only of Leverkühn's life and achievement but also of German history, has deepened and reshaped him to the point where he can embody a humanism stripped of complacency, and at the convulsive end he is fully aware of human actuality and its demonic darkness. Leverkühn soars dangerously as a modernist composer, and neither Zeitblom nor anyone else could have composed his music; yet, Zeitblom, educated in the furthest reaches of music by his friend, is able to report it, and his descriptions of this music play an important, even defining part in the total experience of *Doctor Faustus*. In Germany, Zeitblom observes at one point, "music enjoys the same high popular regard accorded literature in France." Nietzsche, who is a major presence in the background of *Doctor Faustus*, was himself an accomplished musician, incorporated music into his philosophy, and for a while was virtually a collaborator with Wagner. "Without music," said Nietzsche, "life would be a mistake," and music in this novel tells the tale of Faustian Germany.

The importance of Nietzsche to *Doctor Faustus* cannot be emphasized enough. In his essay "Nietzsche's Philosophy in the Light of Modern History," published in 1947, the same year as *Doctor Faustus*, Mann read Nietzsche as the avatar of Adrian Leverkühn. Nietzsche, writes Mann, "was a phenomenon of vast cultural scope and complexity, a veritable résumé of the European spirit." Yet philosophizing "with a hammer [tuning fork]," as he said, he found hollow one thing after another that he admired—Socrates, Jesus, the Enlightenment, Wagner—all unsatisfactory in pursuing original insight and heroic individuality, leaving Zarathustra, alone and self-imagined on his mountaintop, as Mann says,

> like the Alpinist who climbs too high among the glacial peaks until he reaches the point of no return where he can move neither forward nor backward. . . . But what was it that drove Nietzsche upward into the pathless wastes, lashed him to the tortuous climb, and brought him to a martyr's death on the cross of thought?

Mann answers genius, but goes on to a complicated definition of genius as a spiritual disease, which, he adds, in Nietzsche's case was also physical disease, syphilis. Here, Mann takes account of the 1865 letter Nietzsche wrote to his university friend Paul Deussen about his visit to a brothel in Cologne, and also a second visit with the resulting medical record. The syphilis killed him but, Mann understands, contributed to the "glaring white light" of his thought. In a few pages of this essay, Mann gives an outline of the plot of *Doctor Faustus* in terms of Nietzsche, especially that last phrase, "a martyr's death on the cross of thought."

It is with its prose descriptions of Leverkühn's music that *Doctor Faustus* itself becomes a Faustian work of art, pushing beyond the precedents of the novel as a form, breaking out, as will Leverkühn, seeking a freedom beyond, always beyond. It contains, said the novelist John Banville, "some of the greatest unwritten music of the twentieth century, [and] one comes away from it believing that somehow one has heard these works, especially the cantata *Apocalypsis cum figuris* [*Apocalypse with Pictures*]."[4] Music, at the very end of this novel, carries the meaning of the whole, even has the last "word," a word *beyond* language, something vibrating in silence, in Leverkühn's *Lament of Doctor Faustus:*

> Just listen to the ending, listen with me: One instrumental group after the other steps back, and what remains as the work fades away is the high G of a cello, the final word, the final sound, floating off, slowly vanishing in a *pianissimo fermata* [very soft pause]. Then nothing more. Silence and night. But the tone which is no more, for which, as it hangs there vibrating in the silence, only the soul still listens, and which was the dying note of sorrow—is no longer that, its meaning changes, it stands as a light in the night.

At that point, near the end of the novel, we feel that we may be close to our own last chance. Here, Zeitblom's "listen with me" recalls Jesus's "watch with me" to his disciples on the night before his crucifixion. *Doctor Faustus*, then, is a novel necessarily in words but a novel that is trying to become, would rather be, music. "I felt clearly," wrote Mann in *The Story of a Novel*, "that my book itself would have to become the thing it dealt with: namely a musical composition."[5] In this pressure on its own form, *Doctor Faustus* both recounts Leverkühn's excruciating difficulty as a modernist composer and also embodies it in the special predicament of the modernist novel, which suffers the weight of tradition, the older forms worn out and obsolete. Such a novel faces the difficulty of "making it new" as Pound demanded, or as Harry Levin wrote in his *Critical Introduction to Joyce*, "The best writing of our contemporaries is not an act of creation, but an act of evocation, peculiarly saturated with reminiscence. And [Joyce] has enormously increased the difficulty of being a novelist." Mann pushes the novel into music. Breaking out of the form, Mann as author is himself Faust.

Here the prefatory material to *Doctor Faustus* deserves more than a casual glance: Thomas Mann, *Doctor Faustus: The Life of the German Composer, Adrian Leverkühn, as Told by a Friend.* The name Faustus evokes an important European legend, especially a German one. It calls to mind Goethe, but also Marlowe, operas by Gounod and Berlioz, and the late-medieval *Faustbook* with its retelling of legends about the magician who sold his soul to the devil in return for unprecedented powers. The theme itself may go back on the biblical side to Simon the magician in Acts 8, with an immense amount of legendary material added to that, and on the classical side to the dark Titans who warred against the luminous gods on Olympus, including Prometheus, who stole fire from the gods and gave it to mankind, for which he was tortured by Jove. All such stories have as their theme the connection of power and creativity with dark and rebellious powers regarded as coming from "below." In addition, we remember that Oswald Spengler applied the adjective *Faustian* to the entire modern era. Our benign humanist narrator, the "Friend" Serenus Zeitblom, has forgotten too much. He has lost almost all of the European tradition he ostensibly embodies, and when he meets recurrent evils he experiences one shock after another. He resembles most of us more than we care to admit.

On the title page there appear those three proper nouns, "Thomas Mann," "*Doctor Faustus*," and "Adrian Leverkühn." *Doctor Faustus*, printed in the largest type, establishes the paradigm that includes the example of Leverkühn, "German composer"; but Thomas Mann himself must be included here as well, the Faustian writer who pushed this prose work beyond language and into music. And, as we read, Leverkühn is a "German composer." The Faust myth is specifically German, and in this novel Germany is a Faustian nation, infecting itself with the virus of National Socialism as Leverkühn infected himself with syphilis, both of them gaining temporary power and inspiration through a pact with the devil. Neither the name nor the figure of Hitler appears in this novel, but he is a presence nevertheless—no cartoon figure, very far from it, but a presence in Western spirituality. For moral judgments even today Hitler, more than Stalin or Mao, remains the guarantor, maybe the only guarantor, of the actuality of evil. He is never relativized, and a cold wind from the Pit blows through Hitler into our awareness. Along with Mann and Leverkühn, embarrassingly enough, Hitler is an *artist* too, an inspired one, a great orator who sought a German imperial breakthrough parallel to the "breakthrough" of the modernist artist into entirely new forms. Mann drew such a parallel in his essay "Hitler My Brother" (1938). He loathed Hitler, considered him a repellent bohemian, but with a single gift, and who had been able to emerge into politics only through the breakdown of society after the First World War, a good-for-nothing otherwise, but, nevertheless, an artist:

It is ghastly, but it all fits in, as well as many another folk tradition, mingled with debased and pathological elements. . . . Ah, the
artist! . . . For must I not, however much it hurts, regard the man
as an artist-phenomenon? Mortifyingly enough, it is all there. . . .
A brother—a rather unpleasant and mortifying brother. He makes
me nervous, the relationship is painful to a degree. But I will not
disclaim it.

This is grudging, but accurate. Hitler was a mediocre painter, but a great
orator, with access to the deepest emotions of his mass audiences. Listening to recordings of his addresses today, one hears an uncertain beginning,
full of pauses, tentative for a while but then gathering power and rising to
a tremendous crescendo. This reminds the listener of a Wagner overture,
as to *Meistersinger,* and it constitutes a resurrection drama, compelling
in its emotional appeal for a defeated and humiliated Germany after the
First World War.

Though Mann in *Doctor Faustus* calls the Nazi regime the "rule of
the scum," and though there are vast differences in quality among these
Faustian figures, the Faust category encompasses them all. Also in the
prefatory material we hear of the "Friend" of Leverkühn, that is, Serenus
Zeitblom, Mann's narrator, who tells the story of Adrian Leverkühn, and,
while he is telling it between 1943 and 1945, Germany collapses amid
explosions and hellish flames. On the title page, Zeitblom, the "Friend,"
is a much smaller presence, his name not mentioned; nevertheless he is
the pompous, at first verbose, and slightly ridiculous representative of
an enfeebled European humanism—the reader's "Friend," too, in other
words the reader's double, neither of whom are in full possession of the
humanist moral inheritance. Zeitblom will learn and change within the
narrative through his experience of Leverkühn's fate, the fate of Germany,
and his final understanding of the story he tells: "May God have mercy on
your poor soul, my friend, my fatherland." He equates Leverkühn-Faust
with Germany.

A final and very important item in the prefatory material is the epigraph
from Dante, the greatest Christian-classical representative of Renaissance
humanism and, with Homer and Shakespeare, one of the three great poets
of Western civilization. With an ironic smile toward the likely literacy of
his contemporary reader, Mann does not identify this as coming from
canto 2 of the *Inferno.* Nor does he compromise, but gives it in the original Italian. Perhaps he hopes his reader will make the effort to learn some
Italian as part of the reader's own humanistic education. Knowledge, this
novel insists, as does much modernist art, possesses special importance

today. The Renaissance humanists often were teachers by profession, and *Doctor Faustus* is packed with knowledge and implies that we need a great deal more of it than we are likely these days to possess. I will give the important epigraph from the *Inferno* in the Hollander translation:

> Day was departing and the darkened air
> released the creatures of the earth
> from their labors, and I, alone,
>
> prepared to face the struggle—
> of the way and of the pity of it—
> which memory, unerring, shall retrace.
>
> O Muses, O lofty genius, aid me now!
> O Memory, that set down what I saw,
> here shall your worth be shown.

To the Protestant and German north of Faust, Mann adds the Catholic and humanist south. Dante's invocation echoes a similar passage in the *Aeneid* (iii, 147ff.), and by placing this quotation from Dante in his prefatory material, Mann locates himself in the line of Virgil-Dante-Goethe. The invocation to Mnemosyne, goddess of memory and mother of Hesiod's nine Muses of expression, will make acutely real in *Doctor Faustus* the profound truths of hell that we must remember in order to be fully human. Mann's epigraph from the *Inferno,* as we reflect upon it, opens many gates. Mann's story, too, like the *Aeneid* and the *Divine Comedy,* will be a journey, and like both epics but especially Dante's, it will be a journey through hell first, but then, though much more tentatively than in Dante's—our wood is darker and deeper than Dante's and we no longer know our Virgil as guide—we will journey upward and, just possibly, toward the light. With Dante's numinous child Beatrice in mind, one wonders whether Mann will provide an equivalent. He knows that he must do this, and provides one in chapter 44, a virtuoso performance that brings Nepomuk, the divine child, convincingly into this novel, only to have the devil dig his claws into the child's brain and kill him excruciatingly.

The reader, after contemplating its prefatory material, knows that this is a surprisingly learned work. It asks the reader to recover a great deal that has been lost, in that it is a late modernist novel, challenging and intellectually aristocratic. But it is also a traditional humanist work, the early humanists often being educators and learned advisers (Roger Ascham, Thomas More, Castiglione, Machiavelli), and the great humanist works, such at those of Dante, Milton and Goethe, crammed with learning. *Doctor Faustus* belongs directly in that line, its learning apparently inexhaustible.

This vast novel possesses different organizing structures, multiple and interwoven themes. Probably, because most obvious, we should put first the story of Adrian Leverkühn's life and death. Along that time line, the novel creates parallels, including the development of Adrian's music and the history of Germany since Martin Luther. By implication, it includes the history of Renaissance humanism ending with its smashup in 1945, and now attempts the beginnings of repair. Here as a principle of structure we will use Adrian's life, seeing *Doctor Faustus* as forming five distinctive parts analogous to musical movements:

Part 1 (chapters 1–10): The first part introduces Zeitblom as narrator and follows Adrian through his rural childhood and secondary education at Kaisersaschern, a small city, powerfully Gothic in atmosphere. Here, living with his uncle Nikolaus, a craftsman of musical instruments, Adrian awakens to the power of music and attends to the musicology of the local organist Wendell Kretzschmar. Much later, in chapter 25, the devil tells Adrian that where he is, there is Kaisersaschern, and that "we both are very at home in . . . Kaisersaschern, pure Kaisersaschern, good old German air from *anno* fifteen hundred or so, shortly before the arrival of Dr. Martinus, who stood on such stout and cordial terms with me, and threw a hard roll, no, an inkpot, at me, long before the thirty-year [war] festivities."

Part 2 (chapters 11–15): Upon completing his secondary education, Adrian decides to study theology. He attends Halle University, part of Wittenberg, and thus also the alma mater of Luther, Hamlet, and Faust. At Halle he attends the lectures of the Luther-like Professor Ehrenfried Kumpf, and the demonic lecturer on religious psychology Eberhard Schleppfuss ("Dragfoot"). The study of theology does not bring Adrian to or even toward the absolute he seeks, and so he returns to music. In a general way, this parallels Nietzsche's career, from theology and philology to music and philosophy.

Part 3 (chapters 16–19): *This is the center of the novel,* displaced from the physical center in chapter 25 (dialogue with the devil). Now in Leipzig and led by a sinister porter, Adrian visits a bordello and is approached by an attractive prostitute, but flees. He soon traces her to another such establishment in Pressburg, Hungary, where, despite her warning against syphilis, he infects himself. Nietzsche, while a student, visited a bordello in Cologne and may have returned for a second visit; he was infected with syphilis, though certainly not deliberately.[6] Adrian's deliberate self-infection follows immediately upon his decision to pursue music. His relationship with the prostitute eventually issues in a major surprise, a very strange love story. With that infection we have the focus of the emotional and thematic energy of *Doctor Faustus,* with all that follows the inevitable consequence.

Part 4 (chapters 20–42): This is much longer than the previous sections, and inevitably so, because it deals with the manifold results of the infection (Pact with Evil). One result (chapter 25) is the dialogue notably in Palestrina with the triune devil, who explicates the meanings of the pact. By analogy this includes the German fever to "break out" of its central European location that preceded 1914 and, after the social decadence of the 1920s, the infection in its most virulent phase, Nazism, which led to the fiery Götterdämmerung of 1945. In Adrian, analogously, the "inspiration" also results in his masterpiece, the *Apocalypsis cum figuris (Apocalypse with Pictures),* based on a long apocalyptic tradition about last days, including the scriptural book of Revelation, and especially on the sequence of woodcut illustrations of Albrecht Dürer's *Apocalypse.* Performed at Frankfurt in 1926, this oratorio culminates Adrian's musical development in a direction that fuses pure aestheticism with barbarism, and marks the apparent end of Christian humanism as well as the bourgeois era in Europe. The only reviewer to fully understand this great work proves to be a recondite Hungarian musicologist named Madame de Tolna.

Part 5 (chapters 43–47 and epilogue): This brings the agonizing death of Adrian's nephew, the luminous child Nepomuk, whom Adrian loves, and who embodies the nineteenth-century idea of childhood innocence. While Serenus Zeitblom writes this part of the narrative, Germany is being destroyed by the Allies in the west and the Russians from the east, "rushing into despair, into unparalleled bankruptcy . . . descending into hell and the dance of thundering flame." The Allies open the death camps. At a parody Last Supper gathering of many of the characters in the novel, Leverkühn tries to present his last work, *The Lament of Doctor Faustus.* In this he "takes back" Beethoven's Ninth Symphony, with its concluding hymn to joy, music fused with Schiller's poem. This cantata ends with that high G of a cello which echoes and fades in the darkness of despair, an exiguous sound of ultimate hope. Adrian Leverkühn has brought this note to us from the depths of his genius and suffering. He lives on with his brain ruined (again, Nietzsche) for ten years.

Doctor Faustus is energized into novelistic life when Serenus Zeitblom introduces himself in the first two chapters, a man somewhat verbose,

Catholic, the intellectual descendant of the German Renaissance humanists. Born in A.D. 1883, as he puts it, he is two years older than Adrian Leverkühn, whom he has known since childhood. He plays the viola *di amore* (smile from Mann, a viola "of love") and has married a woman named Helene, influenced again humorously, given his conventional personality, by her famous name, but "he is given to things harmonious and reasonable." Serenus lives in the wrong century. He begins the story on May 23, 1943 (the same day Mann began the novel), and his two sons are Nazis, one in the civil service, the other in the armed forces. Things are not going well for Hitler's Fortress Europe. Nor are things altogether reassuring in his account of Adrian's early home in rural Büchel.

Adrian's father, Jonathan Leverkühn, a craftsman with a rural homestead, was "a man of the finest German stamp," and in fact closely resembles Dürer's *Melanchthon*.[7] His physiognomy, Zeitblom says, was "somehow marked by the past, preserved out in the country, so to speak, and brought in from a Germany predating the Thirty Years' War," the Europe-wide Protestant-Catholic war that devastated Germany from 1618 to 1648. In chapter 25, his dialogue with Adrian, the devil refers to this as the thirty-year "festivities," and in their destruction and carnage they were indeed his festivities. We understand that Jonathan Leverkühn is a throwback and theologically on Luther's side. On winter evenings he reads

> a mammoth family Bible bound in smooth pigskin and secured
> with leather clasps, which had been printed around 1700 under the
> license of the Duke of Braunschweig and . . . included the "wise and
> spiritual" prefaces and marginal notes of Dr. Martin Luther.

Luther will be a sinister presence throughout *Doctor Faustus*, being too familiar, we soon understand, with the evil spirit, and we also feel here the gathering and claustrophobic weight of the past, especially the Thirty Years' War. Jonathan Leverkühn has an interest in "nature," or, rather, in natural phenomena that seemingly press beyond the boundaries of nature: inorganic crystals that form plantlike growths when placed in fluids, strange sea animals and shells with apparently cabalistic markings, insects that mimic other insects, and strange moths and butterflies. One such butterfly will provide a major theme in *Doctor Faustus*:

> Its transparent nakedness makes it a lover of dusky, leafy shade, is
> called *Hetaera esmeralda* [prostitute], its wings smudged with just a
> dark smudge of violet and pink, so that in flight, with nothing else
> visible, it imitates a windblown petal.

As he describes these peculiar studies, Zeitblom senses something unpleasant and, though interesting, also *wrong* about them. Jonathan Leverkühn's fascination with the unnatural in nature is Faustian, an interest in magic. Young Adrian shares this in an amused way, and inherits his father's tendency to migraine headaches. He also has a "phenomenal ease" in mastering his grammar school subjects, on whatever subject communicating to his instructor a message of "yes, fine, that much is clear, enough, go on." Even as a child, there is something chilly, even mocking, about him, and he is given to bursts of inappropriate laughter. Because he is so precocious, "at Easter 1895 Adrian left his parents' home and came to town to attend our Boniface Gymnasium [high school]. . . . His uncle, Nikolaus Leverkühn, his father's brother and a respected citizen of Kaisersaschern, consented to take him in." Nikolaus resembles Dürer's portrait of Hieronymus of Augsburg, yet another touch of the pervasive early sixteenth century.[8] He is a master craftsman, a maker of exquisite musical instruments, and it is there, "at the age of fourteen, with the onset of puberty . . . that [Adrian] began to experiment on his own with music on a keyboard in his uncle's house in Kaisersaschern. It was at this time . . . that his inherited migraine began to give him bad days." Father and uncle, magic and music, announce the central theme.

Gothic Kaisersaschern becomes such a force in *Doctor Faustus* that some attention must be paid here to its development as a theme. Here Adrian discovers music, but keeps its attraction for him hidden. According to Zeitblom:

> As far as I can see, he failed to pay [music] any attention back then, or indeed for years afterward, and kept the idea hidden, even from himself, that he might have anything to do with the world of sound. I see it as a subconscious caution on his part; but one can draw on a physiological explanation as well, since it was in fact at the age of fourteen, with the onset of puberty and the emergence from the state of childish innocence, that he began to experiment on his own with music on a keyboard in his uncle's house in Kaisersaschern. It was at this time, by the way, that his inherited migraine began to give him bad days.

We see the conjunction of music with ideas of guilt, the forbidden secrecy, sexuality, loss of innocence, danger sensed. Adrian has kept even "hidden from himself the idea that he might have anything to do with the world of sound." At age fourteen, does he intuit the vast potentialities of pure sound? Zietblom cannot tell us. Perhaps Adrian somehow understands that the "world of sound," unlike those earlier studies that he mastered so effortlessly, has the potentiality of being infinite. As Zeitblom records, "He began to experiment on his own with music on a keyboard in his uncle's house in Kaisersaschern." His migraine, in the last sentence, seems the result of what went before in this sequence of sentences.

The warehouse of instruments that is part of Nikolaus Leverkühn's house has a mysterious and even living quality, in its mass, multiplicity, and mystery, making a sinister impression in Zeitblom's long description. It is "culturally *bewitching*" and "causes one's acoustic *fantasy* to surge and roar" [italics added]. See, for example, a few sentences from a much longer description:

> There lay spread out before one everything that chimes and sings, that twangs, brays, rumbles, rattles and booms—even the keyboard instruments were represented, too, by a celesta with its charming bell-like tones. The *enchanting* violins were hung behind glass or lay bedded in cases that, like *mummy coffins* [italics added] took the shape of their occupants; some were lacquered more yellowish, some more brownish. . . . Leaning there were several specimens of the *violone,* the giant violin, the cumbersome double-bass, capable of majestic recitatives, whose pizzicato is more sonorous than the roll of a tuned kettledrum, and from which one would never expect the veiled magic of its flageolet-like tones.

Given at much greater length in the text, this catalogue of instruments creates an impression of an infinity of sounds, and in its entirety has sinister overtones, a haunted warehouse for Adrian to explore. Outside his uncle's house, there is Kaisersaschern itself, which Zeitblom calls "Lutherland":

> [Kaisersaschern] had preserved a strong sense of the medieval, not just in outward appearances, but also in its atmosphere. The old churches, the faithfully preserved residences and storehouses, buildings with exposed timberwork and projecting upper stories; a city wall with round steepled towers; tree-lined squares paved with cobblestones; a town hall hovering architecturally between Gothic and Renaissance, its roof ornamented by a bell-tower above, loggias below, and two more spires formed bays continuing down the facade to the ground floor—all that establishes a sense of life unbroken in its continuity with the past.

The vague uneasiness already aroused by such a description intensifies:

Its historical museum, which features a chamber with crude instruments of torture, contains a very excellent library of twenty-five
thousand volumes and five thousand manuscripts, among them two
alliterative charms that scholars consider older than those of Mer-
seburg—and of quite harmless import, by the way, conjuring up
more than a little rain in the dialect of Fulda.

In addition to the physical details of Kaisersaschern, there hung in its air
something

of the state of the human heart during the last decades of the fif-
teenth century, a hysteria out of the dying Middle Ages, something
of a latent epidemic, a strange thing to say about a sensibly practical modern town. But it was not modern, it was old, and age is the
past as the present, a past only veneered with the present; and this
may sound bold, but one could imagine a Children's Crusade suddenly erupting there—a St. Vitus' dance, some utopian communistic
lunatic preaching a bonfire of the vanities, miracles and visions of
the Cross, and roving masses of mystic enthusiasts.

Zeitblom writes this in 1943. Suddenly, it occurs to him that right now
he might be living in just such a period. Late medieval Kaisersaschern
fuses in his mind with 1943 Germany. Those old extravagances have not
occurred, he reflects—how could they?

In compliance with the times, the police would not have allowed
it. And yet! What all haven't the police refrained from acting upon
in our own day—again in compliance with the times, which certainly do permit such things of late. Our own times are secretly
inclined—or, rather, anything but secretly, very purposefully in fact,
with a particularly smug sense of purpose that leaves one doubt-
ing life's genuineness and simplicity and perhaps produces a very
false, ill-fated dichotomy—our times are inclined, I say, to return
to such epochs and enthusiastically repeat symbolic actions that
have something sinister about them, that strike in the face of modern understanding: burning books, for instance, and other deeds I
would rather not put into words.

Here Zeitblom's hesitating sentences, his quavering obfuscations, the final
"deeds I would rather not put into words," suggest his own enfeebled
moral sense. What he would "rather not put into words" includes not

only the book burning that he does mention but probably *Kristallnacht* and the extermination camps. Zeitblom is aware of the foul Pit, but even though he is not in danger now himself, he will not mention these directly. Nervously, he will keep what he is writing for another time. In Zeitblom's reflections on Kaisersaschern, we see that interweaving of the deep past with the present that is so effective a feature of this novel. It is the weight of an unassimilated past that in Germany has prevented the emergence of a European humanism and the critical spirit of the Enlightenment. For example, he mentions the contemporary Nazi invocation of the *Volk* (people):

> And here one bold word that comes from the experiences of our own time. For any friend of enlightenment, the word, the concept, of *Volk* always carries some apprehension, and he knows that one has to address the crowd as the *Volk* if one wishes to lure them into some regressive evil. What all has not happened before our eyes—and not just before our eyes either—in the name of the *Volk* that could never have happened in the name of God, or humanity, or of justice. The fact is, however, that the *Volk* is always the *Volk*, at least at a certain level of its being, the archaic level.

Zeitblom half understands that his terms *God, humanity,* and *justice* have lost much of their power. Jacob Burckhardt said that in Voltaire rationalism becomes poetic and even myth, that is, clean like surgical steel as Voltaire sliced through the muck of irrationality. But Zeitblom sees that now the appeal to the *Volk,* antirational and rejecting individuality, possesses spectacular power. Hitler proclaimed that "for us the idea of the *Volk* is higher than the idea of the state." (Perhaps, rather than "higher," he should have said "more fundamental.") On April 6, 1938, Hitler put it this way in a Salzburg speech: "In the beginning was the *Volk,* and only then came the Reich." The Nazi formula made clear that the *Volk* came first: "*Ein Volk, Ein Reich, Ein Führer* [One People, One Nation, One Leader]." The führer supposedly intuited the inarticulate mind of the *Volk* and carried out the demands of that archaic mind, a powerful force connected with blood, soil, and prehistory. Compared with that, the Enlightenment ideas of the individual, the state, the law, and reason possessed a diminished force. In addition, the sense of a great untapped power in the depths of the irrational possesses connections with modernist art: with the buried mind of Europe in *The Waste Land,* the appeal to myth in Joyce and Stravinsky, and to Heidegger seeking Being in the pre-Socratics and still further back. According to Adrian's first mentor in music, the Pennsylvania-born Kaisersaschern organist and theorist Wendell Kretzschmar, there exists a drive in music "to plunge back into the elemental and admire herself in her primitive beginnings." The modernist artist goes back in time, and also down into the powers of the unconscious, seeking to transcend the banal, the ordinary, the used up. Though Hitler loathed modernist art, he was, as Mann uncomfortably saw, also an artist, a great orator, and his appeal to the *Volk* was also an attack on the Enlightenment. As Zeitblom says, Hitler was "fatally inspired." In recordings today we can hear a major Hitler address acting out a Resurrection drama, beginning slowly, hesitantly, gradually gaining in force as if drawing power from the massed audience before him, the *Volk*, and finally rising to a thunderous climax of fury, determination, and aggressive power. There can be no doubt that he turned into oratory such passages from Wagner as the prelude to *Meistersinger*—about which, not incidentally, Nietzsche wrote brilliantly in *Beyond Good and Evil*. Hitler's slogan was *"Deutschland erwache!"* ("Germany Awaken!"), as if from the tomb, and this appeal to a Germany defeated and humiliated in 1918 had the force that turned variegated individual Germans, shopkeepers, professionals, businessmen, farmers, and *Brauhaus* (brew house) froth blowers into an awakened *Volk*, a force that was re-created at least in Hitler's mind as a vast mythic cohort of Nordic warriors. Hitler was an artist, a magician, a *Zauberer* (wizard). In the bunker, facing defeat and suicide, he considered that the German people had let the Reich down— as imagined *Volk* and imagined *Reich* it could be said that they had not played their assigned parts in his unwritten opera. Analysts of social forms classify National Socialism as "neo-traditionalism," elements of the past made effective by modern methods: autobahns, blitzkriegs, rockets, the *Volk*, the German "soil." For many sensitive spirits, the "German Revolution," initially at least, had great appeal.

At first Adrian's attraction to the "world of sound" seems to be merely intuitive. Kretzschmar renders it analytical and cerebral, a matter of increasingly complex problems that demand to be solved. As we might expect from his performance in school, Adrian breezes through these, always with a driving cerebral desire for more problems and more solutions.

The local organist in Kaisersaschern, and a public lecturer on music for the edification of the local community, Kretzschmar was born in Pennsylvania, but has returned to the Germany of his grandparents. His lectures sometimes are crippled by an uncontrollable stutter. Under his influence young Adrian penetrates high theory. Zeitblom recalls that it was probably *between Greek and trigonometry classes,* as he leaned against an abutment of the glazed brick wall in the school yard, that he told me about these magical amusements of his leisure time: about the transformation of the intervals within a chord (which occupied him more than anything else), of the horizontal, that is, into the vertical, of the sequential into the simultaneous. Simultaneity, he claimed, was in fact the primary factor, for each note, with its closer and more distant overtones, was itself a chord, and the scale was entirely sound spread out analytically in horizontal sequence. [italics added]

The italicized phrase possesses metaphorical quality, movement from classics (humanism) to the abstract, the latter associated with musical theory ("magical amusements").

Here Mann begins that technical realization of music that will carry through Adrian's life as a composer. And, as he said in *Story of a Novel, Doctor Faustus* needed not only to describe music but, importantly, to become music, with the result that words fuse with sound that carries the meaning.

Adrian, fascinated by music in its technical actuality, sees it as cerebral, problems to be solved. At the same time, with Kretzschmar, he was gaining in skill as a pianist: "For a while as a pianist he was rapidly, indeed almost too hastily and taxingly, gaining a perhaps incoherent but often intensely detailed general overview of preclassical, classical, romantic, and modern late-Romantic composition (and not just those of German origin but also Italian, French, Slavic)." He comes to see music as driven by a succession of problems posed and solved, driven always to transcend itself:

> "Bach's problem," he said, "was this: 'How can one create polyphony that is harmonically meaningful?' For the moderns, the question presents itself somewhat differently. It is more like, 'How can one create harmony that has the appearance of polyphony?' Strange how it looks like a bad conscience—homophonic music's bad conscience in the presence of polyphony."

There, music, like a human being, can have a "conscience," and a bad one if it does not follow the logic of its own development: and the logical development of the homophonic is the polyphonic.

Pursuing that process of reasoning, one must reach an end—the furthest possible point of musical possibility. Or, must one? All valid art

possesses originality, but must it be radical originality? Ben Jonson's lyrics
are as timeless as those of Catullus. Cannot fresh experience be expressed
in a sestina? Surely it is possible to write a new and good song. No,
not in a Faustian world. While such a fine composer as Aaron Copland,
who had studied in Paris and was familiar with modernism, elected to
stay with more traditional forms, as in *Appalachian Spring*, that is not
possible in the world of modernist art, where the new, the solutions to
solutions, drives toward the radical, the energetic transcendence of the
latest solution.

By the end of his years in Kaisersaschern, Adrian has already probed
into the nature of music. As Zeitblom summarizes it, music

> was the most intellectual of all the arts, which was evident in the
> fact that in music as in no other art, form and content were inter-
> twined, were absolutely one and the same. One might say, "Music
> appeals to the ear": but it did so only in a qualified sense—that is,
> only in those instances where hearing, like any other sense, acted as
> the conduit, the receptive organ for the intellectual content. But in
> fact there was music that did not reckon at all with being heard . . .
> it was music per se, music as pure abstraction.

Adrian now reaches the point where he has begun to think about
greatness in music. He says to Kretzschmar that German music exhibits

> a manifestation of highest energetic will—in no way abstract, but
> lacking an object, energetic will in pure space, in the clear ether—and
> where does that occur a second time in the universe! We Germans
> have acquired the term per se from philosophy and use it every day
> without intending anything very metaphysical. But here you have it,
> music like this is energetic will, energetic will per se—not as an idea,
> but in its reality. I offer for your consideration that this is almost a
> definition of God. *Imitatio Dei.* I'm amazed it's not forbidden.

Given this will and this theoretical ambition, it is not surprising that
Adrian runs into a conceptual wall. Zeitblom concludes chapter 9 and
Adrian's years in Kaisersaschern with the summation, "A massive dose
of musical knowledge—and his own excited participation in it—became
part of his life in those days, only to come then for years to what at least
appeared to be a total standstill." Yet we know that his intellectual ambition and the will that drives it cannot rest at a standstill, merely repeating,
however skillfully, what has already been accomplished.

✦

In the structure outlined earlier, part 2 (chapters 11–15) brings Adrian to the University of Halle. The reader should not be surprised that having reached a standstill in music he now studies theology, the "study of god(s)." Though pursuing the demonic theme already established at Kaisersaschern, this sequence lightens it considerably with elements of humor. This university, it turns out, is "identical with the university of Wittenberg, since the two were joined upon their reopening at the end of the Napoleonic Wars." Among Adrian's famous predecessors at Wittenberg thus were Luther, Faustus, and Prince Hamlet—this is not Princeton— three of the most conspicuous figures in the Western mind. As we enter it with Leverkühn, Luther, Melanchthon, and Hutten seem always just down the hall or around the next medieval corner.

Here, Professor Ehrenfried Kumpf, a "rugged" figure, is a comical Luther and speaks old-fashioned German. His "liberalism" is based not on a humanistic distrust of dogma, but on a religious distrust of the reliability of our thinking. This does not "prevent him from a sturdy faith in revelation or, what is more, from being on intimate, though very strained terms with the Devil." Luther himself is said to have thrown his inkwell at the devil. Professor Kumpf at a dinner party throws a hard roll at a shadowy corner of the dining room. (This kind of thing is by no means absent from the modern academy. A famous Samuel Johnson scholar was known to keep bits of orange peel in his pocket, as did the lexicographer; and at least one Virginia Woolf scholar resembles in many ways the subject of her research.)

Another academic figure here may be a bit more menacing than Kumpf. Eberhard Schlepfuss, lecturer on "The Psychology of Religion," wore a "floppy hat" and "would doff it with a long sweep of the hand and say, 'Your very humble servant, sir.' " Traditionally, Dragfoot is one name for the devil, and Dragfoot the lecturer has a "small forked beard" and "splintersharp teeth set between it and his tapered and twirled moustache." The doctrine this man teaches is far from comical. Evil, he maintains, is inseparable from the creation, there at the beginning, and "the procreative act, marked by aesthetic hideousness, was both the expression and the vehicle of original sin—what wonder then, that the Devil had been left an especially free hand in the matter? It was not for nothing that the angel had said to Tobias: 'The demon hath power to overcome those who lust.' " This teaching by Schlepfuss seems demonic—repellent and probably evil in its loathing, and should not, it hardly need be said, be taken at face value, omitting as it does a more humane, indeed humanistic, view of sexuality.

This section ends with Leverkühn, having tried theology, such as it was at Halle, returning to music and Wendell Kretzschmar, who finds him advancing beyond the instructor, "uncovering connections between motifs" and perceiving "the division of a short segment into question and answer, as it were, and [he] can see in general and from inside how it's done."

Ambiguously, if comically, Leverkühn's experience at Halle, where theology has fallen short, leads to the central episode of *Doctor Faustus*. In part 3 (chapters 16–19) Mann establishes a credibly profound transgression that follows through the rest of *Doctor Faustus,* for Adrian himself and, by analogy, for Germany. It provides the "breakthrough" for his music and, intertwined with it, a fatal love story (in its interpolated form an old-fashioned story-within-the-story that is not complete until the final page of the novel).

The year is 1905. Zeitblom has undertaken his required military service and Adrian has moved to Leipzig. He visits two brothels, the first inadvertently and misled by a disreputable porter, and describes it to Zeitblom in a letter composed in Luther-like German, resembling except for that imitation a letter written by Nietzsche in 1865 to his friend Paul Deussen, a fellow university student. As Adrian describes it, he enters a *faux* luxurious parlor with "silken couches, upon which there sit waiting for you the nymphs and daughters of the wilderness, six or seven—how shall I put it—*morphos, clearwings, esmeraldas,* scantily clad." He remembers, writing this, the strange, the "unnatural" butterfly that fascinated his father, the *Hetaera esmeralda.* Instantly, he flees to a piano, whereupon, "There steps to my side a nut-brown lass, in Spanish jacket, with large mouth, stubbed nose, and almond eyes—Esmeralda, who strokes my cheek with her arm." Adrian flees the bordello. He has made the connection between this prostitute and the sinister butterfly *Hetaera esmeralda,* recalled now by the reader as one whose transparent nakedness makes it a lover of dusky, leafy shade, its wings smudged with just a splash of violet and pink, so that in flight, with nothing else visible, it imitates a windblown petal.

Here is the relevant passage in Nietzsche's 1865 letter to Paul Deussen:

> I found myself surrounded by a half a dozen apparitions in tinsel and gauze, looking at me expectantly. For a short time I was speechless. Then I made instinctively for the piano as being the only soulful thing present. I struck a few chords, which freed me from my paralysis, and I escaped.

It is not certain that Nietzsche visited a second brothel and there infected himself, as Leverkühn will do, yet it is agreed that Nietzsche, like Leverkühn, died of syphilis. Nietzsche, much more than Beethoven and Wagner, who were also touched by the demonic, haunts *Doctor Faustus* as the principal paradigm of the artist. Adrian resembles Nietzsche in precocious intellect, asceticism, chronic illness and migraine headaches, impatient academic career, sense of chilly aloneness, and fierce aspiration. Indeed, Nietzsche's philosophizing has more the character of art than of discourse as he adopts one philosophical mode after another, even identifying himself with Jesus as the self-crucified, and, at the end, alone on his spiritual mountain peak, as Zarathustra, speaking inspired and unwanted truths.

That, however, is a particular kind of genius, the Faustian. In *Doctor Faustus* the traditional, it might be called healthy, genius—Chaucer, Shakespeare, Bach, Handel, Mozart, Goethe—that is, the central and normal, is finished, at least for now. The accumulation of past achievement now bears down too heavily, the strain on the artist to achieve originality has become too great, and the artist must make a "breakthrough" to the new. In addition, the artist is related to his surrounding society, and Leverkühn's Germany, from the period before the First World War, was itself afflicted by a "fever" and, as strange things happened, sought a "breakthrough" to world power. If wholeness of spirit is to be achieved, it must be re-earned, and the journey is difficult in the extreme.

Adrian's letter to Zeitblom describing his visit to the brothel therefore necessarily has two parts. As soon as he finishes the brothel scene, he drops the Luther-like German and abruptly discusses music in a highly analytical way. A relationship between the two parts is implied by the juxtaposition. The advance of music requires the former. Zeitblom penetrates the Luther-like language as a way of masking seriousness while at the same time revealing a visit to a "hell-hole of lusts," as Adrian frankly calls it. Zeitblom, now astutely in this as in much else, and reflecting his development from the original narrator, observes that "the arrogance of the intellect had suffered the trauma of an encounter with soulless instinct," and intuiting that "Adrian would return to the spot where his deceiver [the shady guide] had led him." Yes, but the first visit to the brothel was more complex than an encounter of "arrogance of intellect" with "soulless instinct." The prostitute proved to be very far from soulless.

As Zeitblom foresees, Adrian does return a year later to the prostitute. He writes Zeitblom to say that he had sought out the woman at the same bordello, but had found that she "had left to undergo hospital treatment." Undeterred by that warning, he traced her to Pressburg in Hungary, where there occurred a remarkable encounter. Zeitblom's narration in chapter 19 warrants quotation at some length because of its centrality to the entire novel, raising as it does the question of why Adrian sought out this evidently dangerous *Hetaera esmeralda*. Zeitblom finds the entire subject daunting, but is consoled

> by the thought that something resembling the bond of love reigned here, lending some shimmer of human soul to the union of this precious young man with that ill-fated creature.

Though it seems unlikely that Adrian might somehow have loved the prostitute from whom he had fled, this cannot be ruled out. But, Zeitblom continues:

> To be sure, this comforting thought is linked inseparably to another, all the more dreadful one: that here, once and for all, love and poison were joined in a single experience, as a mythological unity embodied in the arrow.

In other words a *Liebestod* (love-death). But, then, did the "creature" respond to that higher impulse?

> It would appear that the poor creature's heart had feelings that responded to those the young man extended to her. There is no doubt she recalled her transient visitor from a year before. Her approaching him to stroke his cheek with her bared arm may have been the vulgarly tender expression of her susceptibility for everything that set him apart from her usual clientele.

Since she is dealing with a genius, that may understate it. He is not merely "different from her usual clientele." Qualitatively, he is stranger and higher. But then, we hear,

> She learned from his own lips that he had made this long journey for her sake, and she thanked him—by warning him against her body. I know this from Adrian himself. She warned him; and does that not imply a gratifying disparity between the creature's higher humanity and that physical part of her, the vile commodity of trade cast to the gutter? The hapless woman warned the man who desired

her against "herself" and that means an act of the soul freely elevating itself above her pitiful physical existence, a humane act of distancing herself from it, an act of compassion, an act, if I may be permitted the word of love.

That may indeed be adequate to this moment as seen from her side, a transformation brought about by Adrian's seeking her out, seeing her as valuable in some way beyond her customary existence. Yes, but, if so, what was it that brought Adrian here to her in Pressburg? Zeitblom now struggles to understand:

And, good heavens, was it not love as well—or what was it, what act of obsession, what act of will recklessly tempting God, what impulse to incorporate the punishment in the sin, or finally, what most deeply seated desire to receive and conceive the demonic, to unleash a deadly chemical change within his own body was it—that caused him, though warned, to spurn the warning and insist on possessing that flesh?

At that moment, Zeitblom begins to understand the story he himself has been telling. By returning to the prostitute as he did, Adrian proved to her that she mattered, that she had a more fully human possibility. Yes, but Adrian also sought something more complicated. Zeitblom says, "I have never been able to think of that encounter without a religious shudder—for in that embrace, one party forfeited his salvation, the other found hers." Yet did he "forfeit his salvation"? Or did he stand in relation to the prostitute as Jesus did to Mary Magdalene—since at the end of the novel Adrian is, in effect, crucified?

However that may be, in deliberately infecting himself with syphilis, Adrian decisively separated himself from health and normalcy, gained a "deadly chemical change within his own body" to which he owes his "breakthrough" as a composer, a breakthrough in solving those complex musical problems where each solution represents an advance on the absolute. He owes the fulfillment of his genius to this woman and her infection and, as Zeitblom explains, incorporates his name for her in his greatest music. Her name,

the one he had given her from the beginning—haunts his work like a rune, legible to no one but me. . . . Within my friend's tonal tapestry there is a conspicuously frequent use of a figure, a sequence of five or six notes, that begins with an H . . . and ends on an Es . . . with E and

> A alternating in between—a basic motif with an oddly melancholy
> sound that pervades his music in a variety of harmonic and rhythmic
> disguises, assigned now to one voice, now to another . . . and then
> in the late work, with its unique blend of boldness and despair, most
> especially in *Lament of Doctor Faustus,* which was written in Pfei-
> ffering and displays to an even greater extent a tendency to present
> those melodic intervals in harmonic simultaneity. And that encoded
> sound reads as: H-E-T-A-E-R-A: *Hetaera esmeralda.*

She chemically inspires Leverkühn's music by infecting him, and she
becomes his music as he incorporates her into it. Remarkably, the prostitute of Pressburg one day will herself come to understand this.

At this point, the tone of the narrative greatly lightens as the more
immediate results of Adrian's infection appear as virtual farce, but with
dangerous overtones. Five weeks after his visit to *Haetera esmeralda* he
comes down with a "local infection." The first physician he visits, a Dr.
Erasmi, prescribes a "rather lengthy therapy," but almost immediately
drops dead. Of course this is coincidental, but . . . is it? We may think
that the original Erasmus was too irenic a humanist to deal with Luther.
Perhaps more than Luther. A second physician, a Dr. Zimbalist, treated
Adrian twice, but then was led away handcuffed, apparently a criminal.
Something mysterious is resisting a cure for Leverkühn's syphilis. In fact
bad—usually fatal—things happen to those who have enjoyed his affec-
tion or try to befriend him.

Part 4 of the five parts of the novel (chapters 20–42) is by far the longest,
dealing as it does with the results of the demonic in Leverkühn's life and
music. It must be capacious, because he has been established as a representative figure, in fact the representative figure of his era for Mann,
the metaphor for Germany, and an example that is both instructive and
potentially redeeming for the civilization of the West. What happens to
Leverkühn in part 4 has happened to Germany and may also reflect the
dark side of Western civilization.

Now, as this extensive part of the novel begins, all of the principal elements of *Doctor Faustus* are firmly in place, and what remains before the
denouement in part 5 and the final cantata, *Lament for Doctor Faustus,* is
to see how these elements play out. There will be one major surprise. But,
in the end, everything has a sense of inevitability; it may be providential
inevitability. The feeling of a hidden drive or, as it were, undertow, is powerful throughout this part of the novel. We may conveniently summarize
its thematic elements as follows:

a) After Adrian Leverkühn's deliberate self-infection on his second brothel visit, he "breaks out" into the full development of his genius culminating in his oratorio, the *Apocalypsis cum figuris*, first performed at Frankfurt in 1926. A masterpiece of modernism, it is hailed by some but execrated by many. The apocalypse is that of the European bourgeois era, which ultimately will end amid flame and horror.

b) Though Adrian rejected the bourgeois and the normal with his infection, that is, sealed his pact with the devil in order to achieve his musical breakthrough, the novel now presents in chapter 25 his dialogue with the devil(s) in Palestrina, Italy, a Trinity of devil figures amounting to one devil. In its negative analogy with Christianity, this dialogue represents Adrian's "confirmation" after his "first communion" in the bordello. The devil(s) provides an explication of the meaning of the pact.

c) Earlier, *Doctor Faustus* has reached back to the late Middle Ages, to Luther and the Thirty Years' War; now, in part 4, woven through the narrative, we have the history of Germany from about 1900 through the 1930s, and there, as Zeitblom puts it, the Nazi "rule of the scum." The demonic virus has fatally infected Germany, and the national apocalypse—the last days of 1945—approaches.

d) The morale of the upper bourgeoisie has constituted a distinctive theme in Mann beginning with *Buddenbrooks* (1924), and it is central to *Doctor Faustus*. When the upper middle class loses its sense of responsibility, grave danger threatens its civilization. We may see this conviction reflected in the rigid persona of Mann himself, impeccable haute bourgeois in appearance and manner, a responsible burgher, but his rigidity asserted against his artist within, who from his early years was drawn to an assortment of complex and dangerous emotions. In trying to perpetrate an absurd swindle in which a mouse is supposed to eat its way out of an insured parcel, one Gleichen-Russwurm, a descendant of Schiller's, is caught and disgraced. Zeitblom blames the "general moral confusion" of the Weimar period for this lunatic scheme.

In this long part 4 two events stand out as both striking in themselves and of the first importance, the dialogues with the devil(s) in chapter 25 and the completion and performance of *Apocalypsis cum figuris* in 1926 (chapter 36).

In 1912, Adrian has spent a working vacation with his friend the translator Rüdiger Schildknapp in Palestrina, Italy, the birthplace of the composer and also, Zeitblom tells us, known to the ancients as Praeneste. Zeitblom adds, with a striking piece of erudition, that Praeneste (Dante's Penestrino) is mentioned in canto 27 of the *Inferno*. Though that brief reference might seem trivial, it introduces one of the innumerable bits of relevant learning with which Mann enriches the texture of *Doctor Faustus*. Dante sees Praeneste (Palestrina) as a stronghold of the French king's attack on Pope Boniface VIII. Though Dante judged Boniface to have been a great sinner, and placed him far down among the simoniac damned in *Inferno* 19, Boniface was also God's vicar; the military attack on him by the French king using Palestrina as a base for French military action against him was an abomination. Palestrina thus is associated with evil as well as with the composer, perhaps another "inspired" composer. Mann's ideal reader enjoys ferreting such things out, and when they are brought to the surface they add to the richness and authority of the narrative.

It is about five years after Adrian's infection with syphilis that the devil(s) appear to him in Palestrina, evidently comfortable there, in view of the history to which Dante alludes. The episode also recalls Ivan Karamazov's analogous dialogue. It seems possible that the infection has flared up and is affecting Adrian's sanity. He describes the experience for Zeitblom on sheets of music paper written in an "ornate monkish hand." Whether the devil(s) exist outside Adrian's diseased mind Zeitblom leaves an open question, though the manifestation coincides with a sudden drop in room temperature. The devil(s) in order of appearance resemble a spindly and shabby pimp, then change into a bespectacled music theorist in white collar and bow tie, and finally into a theologian with a small forked beard who resembles Schlepfuss, the lecturer at Halle. These represent individuals who have been important in Adrian's introduction to the demonic. The pimp discourses on disease, lovingly mentions "the flagellates, the tiny imperceptible sort . . . the *spirocheta pallida* of syphilis," the stimulus for creativity, and he understands that "disease creates a certain critical opposition to the mediocre life, disposes a man to be obstinate and ironical so that he seeks refuge in free thought. . . . One ought not, my boy, leave to the suburbanite the final word as to what is sick and healthy."

The devil-as-critic understands that while "the masterpiece, the structure in equilibrium, belongs to traditional art, emancipated art disavows it," and, exploring the technical requirements, he proclaims, requires that "conventions once prerequisite and compulsory" must now be discarded to reach the intrinsic goals of composition: "Every better composer now bears within him a canon of the forbidden," that is, of the traditional and classical. All of this has already been made plain in *Doctor Faustus,* and this devil-as-critic is a theorist of modernism. But he now changes into a third form and begins to speak theologically, resembling Schlepfuss, and adds something important. Under modern conditions, he says, in which banal liberal humanitarianism rules, evil becomes the last guarantee of the absolute: "Who else, I would like to know, should speak to you today of religion? Surely not the liberal theologian? I am by now the only one who preserves it!" (Thus today, as earlier has been said here, Hitler testifies to evil, and is our indispensable metaphysical absolute. Neither Stalin nor Mao quite serves the purpose, even though they piled up more corpses.)

It is in the dialogue with the third manifestation, the devil-as-theologian, Schlepfuss, that the theology of the novel becomes clarified. Adrian proves the better theologian than the lecturer at Halle, who insists that *contritio* (repentance) is excluded for him, that he is already in hell right now. Not so fast, Adrian replies:

> I would warn you not to feel all too sure of me. A certain shallowness in your theology could tempt you to it. You depend on my pride's preventing me from the remorse necessary to salvation, yet do not make account of there being a prideful remorse—that of Cain, who was of the fast opinion that his sin was greater than could e'er be forgiven him. . . . You will admit that grace can have only a workaday concern for the workaday sinner. In his case the act of grace has little impulsion, is but a dull enterprise. Mediocrity has no theological life whatsoever. A sinfulness so hopeless that it allows its man fundamentally to despair of hope is the true theological path to salvation.

Paul and Augustine, not to mention the prodigal son, are near at hand: it is experiencing the depths, hell itself, knowing how bad things are, that makes the sinner most feel the need for salvation.

Modernism in art represents an art of the extremes, and Adrian has expounded the theology of modernism. Thus Celia in Eliot's *Cocktail*, dying the death of a saint on an anthill, achieves salvation—rather than the ordinary cocktail party sorts—and in *Four Quartets* the sinner must be redeemed from fire by fire: only then is it possible for the fire and the rose to be one. Not all modernism, of course, is theological, but it is always difficult, always excludes and shuns the ordinary and the mediocre, and always refines its special audience of the "saved," even if saved only in a secular and cultural sense. Modernism is an art of the saving remnant. For secular as well as theological modernism, a pervasive mass culture is the aesthetic hell, the condition furthest from aesthetic salvation, and rightly so.

✦

The devil's appearance in 1911 or thereabouts leads in the time line of Adrian's life through a sense of decadence in the Munich upper middle class, which mixes bohemianism and art, until in August 1914 the novel reaches the First World War, which Zeitblom describes as accompanied by excitement, reaching fever proportions and widely seen as breaking through "to a new form of life in which state and culture will be one." This description has obvious parallels to the development of Adrian's music, in which his infection gives him the impetus to break through into a new form or forms of music. The First World War will not in fact issue in "a new form of life in which state and culture are one." That leap beyond Enlightenment to the fusion of culture and politics will be postponed until the advent of the Third Reich.

Meanwhile, along Adrian's time line, the 1920s bring a feeble if well-intentioned Weimar Republic, but with it a more radical decadence of the upper bourgeoisie, epitomized by the Kridwis circle in Munich. But also during this postwar period Adrian's musical composition moves from one modernist achievement to another, his own breakthroughs representing a surge of creativity no doubt energized by the toxic infection released into his system.

Chapter 34 brings his *Apocalypse*. His culminating work, it draws on a Christian apocalyptic tradition embodied in the Book of Revelation and a great deal of subsequent art, especially Albrecht Dürer's seventh woodcut in his famous series that, as we hear, shows a disturbing "density of space filled with fantastically precise detail." Leverkühn's homage to Dürer is shown by the title of his oratorio, *Apocalypsis cum figuris*. This high modernist oratorio reminds Zeitblom of "how close aestheticism prepares for barbarism in one's own soul." This is a much changed Serenus Zeitblom from the one met in the early chapters. Now, with chapter 34, the novel fulfills the goal toward which it has been tending since Adrian's early technical exercises with Wendell Kretzschmar in Kaisersaschern. It fuses language with music, *becomes* music, and the music itself recapitulates much that has gone before.[9] Perhaps a very few quotations from this virtuoso description will suffice to give a sense of the extended passage:

> There are ensembles that begin as speaking choruses and only by stages, by way of the oddest transitions, arrive at the richest vocal music; choruses, that is, that move through all the shades of graduated whispering, antiphonal speech, and quasi-chant on up to the

most polyphonic song—accompanied by sounds that begin as simple noise, as magical, fanatical, African drums and booming gongs, only to attain the highest music.

The sliding tone . . . whose images of terror certainly supply the most enticing, and at the same time legitimate reasons for employing this wild device. In the passage where four voices from the altar order the four avenging angels to be let loose to slay horses and riders, emperor and pope, and a third part of mankind, trombone glissandi represent the theme and the devastating slide across the instrument's seven positions is used to terrifying effect! The howl as a theme—how ghastly!

This sardonic *gaudium* of Gehenna as it sweeps across fifty bars, beginning with the giggle of a single voice, only to spread rapidly to seize choir and orchestra, then, amid rhythmic upheavals and counterblows and jettisons, to swell to a horrible fortissimo tutti, to a dreadful mayhem of yowls, yelps, screeches, bleats, bellows, howls and whinnies, to the mocking, triumphant laughter of hell.

Not surprisingly, the 1926 premiere of the *Apocalypse* in Frankfurt evokes audience rebellion characteristic of reactions to modernist art, as Zeitblom records: "It goes without saying this [production] did not happen without angry protests and loud, embittered claims that art was being mocked, a musical crime perpetrated." *The Waste Land* had been dismissed in such terms, although the appreciative John Peale Bishop, for example, described it as "immense, magnificent, terrible" and said that some lines "make my flesh creep."[10] Leverkühn's *Apocalypse* too receives an extended analysis that is profoundly aware of its greatness and meaning, in the avant-garde periodical *Abruch,* the author one "Desiderius [Erasmus?] Fehér," who turns out to be a Hungarian musicologist and cultural philosopher. Fehér writes fervently about "the high intellectual level and religious content, the pride and the despair, the sinful cleverness of a music driven toward pure inspiration." He speculates with embarrassment that he "had not discovered this most intriguing and thrilling music on his own, had not chanced upon it at the behest of a bidding from within, but rather had to be guided to it from outside," or, as he said, from above, from a "a sphere higher than academia, from the sphere of love and faith, in a word, by the eternal feminine."

In a surprising development, Adrian soon learns that the author of this remarkable essay, conscious of the inspiration of the "eternal feminine," was actually a woman, a Hungarian named Madame de Tolna. Zeitblom writes that no novelist would dare introduce the rest of this story into his narrative, and that neither he nor Adrian ever saw Madame de Tolna, but goes on to describe the strange relationship she develops with Adrian. The widow of a dissolute and diseased Hungarian aristocrat, she has inherited his wealth and his estates; ill herself, she has a physician constantly in attendance, though she travels extensively, and has visited every locality associated with Leverkühn. She invites him to vacation at her magnificent Tolna Castle, but she is always absent during his visit. She possesses expert knowledge of his music and has sent him a ring, a splendid piece of Renaissance art, which he always wears as he composes. The device on this ring consists of a serpent whose tongue is shaped like a dart. The alert reader may recall that in describing Adrian's second visit to the prostitute in Pressburg, Hungary, that Zeitblom had written of their embrace how "here, once and for all, love and poison were joined as a single experience, as a mythological unity embodied in the arrow." All of these details, and also some etymological clues, lead to the conclusion that Madame de Tolna can be none other than *Hetaera esmeralda*, the nut-brown, snub-nosed prostitute of Leipzig, and that she is now in Hungary, probably still syphilitic, and has infected her dead Hungarian aristocratic husband. But, with the exotic Renaissance ring, she confirmed and sealed her spiritual marriage to Adrian. Their embrace had inspired his rise to greatness and, with his example of spiritual nobility, had also inspired her rise out of the Hungarian brothel and to intellectual achievement, as reflected in her article on Leverkühn's *Apocalypse*.[11] Mann has dared to use the cliché of the virtuous prostitute and has succeeded in accomplishing something remarkable with it.

In the relatively brief but wrenching part 5, which, twenty-four years after the infection, culminates in *The Lament of Doctor Faustus* and then Leverkühn's collapse into Nietzschean-syphilitic dementia, juxtaposed in the narrative with the fiery 1945 Götterdämmerung of Germany, Mann redeems another sentimental cliché, the nineteenth-century ideal of the beautiful and innocent child. With Adrian's angelic nephew Nepomuk Schweigestil, Mann succeeds again against the grain (chapters 44–45). Nepomuk's beauty and power become credible through his own words and through the way people react to him:

> Nepomuk, or "Nepo" as his family called him, or "Echo," as with a whimsical bungling of the consonants, he had called himself when he first began to babble, was dressed in a very simple summer outfit, nothing one would call city clothes: a white cotton short-sleeved

shirt, very brief linen shorts, and well-worn leather shoes on his bare feet. Nevertheless, to behold him was the same as if one were gazing at an elfin prince. . . . A visitor from some tinier, daintier, finer world. . . .

He brought something close to bliss, a constant and cheering and tender warming of the heart, not just to the farm, but to the village as well, even to the town of Waldshut. . . . He folded his hands— held up a little distance from his face—and recited a prayer for the pastor of Pfeiffering, a queer old prayer, that began with the words, "There be no aid against timeful death"; and the man was so moved that he could only say, "Ah, thou babe of God, thou blessed one!" and pat the boy's head with a white priestly hand and give him a brightly colored picture of the Lamb. And the teacher, as he told it later, had felt himself "a different man" when talking to him.

"Echo"—unaware, he names himself after sound—suggests holy inspiration to everyone who knows him, perhaps like the holy child Dante had seen in the streets of Florence. Leverkühn had loved the violinist Rudi Schwerdtfeger, who then was murdered; now, Nepo is his last love. He "liked to walk hand in hand with him across the fields . . . from the first day he dearly loved his little nephew . . . the boy's arrival had brought a radiant daylight into his life." As Mann said in *The Story of a Novel,*

> I took the tenderness of my own heart and transformed it into something no longer entirely rational, endowing the child with a loveliness which was somehow divine, so that people felt him as a visitor from some high and faraway realm, an epiphany.[12]

Of course Nepomuk must die, the man of the "cold" must not be permitted to love him. He must die now, through meningitis, a disease of the nervous system (like syphilis) that is excruciating for the beautiful child and wrenching for the exhausted reader. When Zeitblom tries to comfort Leverkühn, the composer suddenly and unexpectedly cries,

> Spare yourself, spare yourself and make the sign of the cross! Things are happening up there. Make it not only for yourself, but for me too, and for my guilt! What guilt, what a sin, and what a crime . . . that we let him come, that I let him get near me, that I let my eyes feast on him! Surely you know that children are made of delicate stuff, are all too receptive to poisonous influences.

As Nepo dies, the child's face distorted in devilish agony, Leverkühn says,

> I have discovered that it ought not to be . . . the good and noble.
> What people have fought for, have stormed citadels for, and have
> announced with jubilation—it ought not to be. It will be taken
> back. I will take it back. . . . the Ninth Symphony.

Beethoven, Schiller's "Ode to Joy" at the end of the Ninth Symphony, music
and words together hailing the triumph of enlightenment and humanity,
the very pinnacle of nineteenth-century optimism, all this is gone, all of
it now mere illusion. Leverkühn is not an unbeliever. He is certain about
hell. He had only seemed to reach the bottom in his great *Apocalypse* oratorio with its hellish cacophonies. That was cultural despair expressed in
his peak of musical achievement. With the death of Nepomuk and his own
supposed complicity he has reached the bottom below the bottom. As
Milton wrote of his Satan, "In the lowest depth a still lower depth opened
wide." Or, as Heidegger said of the syphilitic Nietzsche in the year 1887,
"Everything about him radiates an excessive brilliance and . . . at the same
time a terrible boundlessness advances out of the distance."

Mann must produce a powerful ending for *Doctor Faustus* in order to
justify the expectations that have been built by all that has gone before.
He succeeds impressively in the final two chapters, 46 and 47.

The former begins in the present time of the Zeitblom narrative, the
flames, blood, and shattering explosions as the Third Reich dies in 1945,
our "thick-walled torture chamber, into which Germany was transformed
by a vile regime of conspirators sworn to nihilism from the very start."
Hell indeed becomes opened to daylight:

> A transatlantic general has the inhabitants of Weimar file past the
> crematoria of their local concentration camp and declares (should
> we say unjustly?) that they, citizens who went about their business
> in seeming honesty and tried to know nothing, though at times the
> wind blew the stench of burned human flesh up their noses, declares
> that they share in the guilt for these horrors that are now laid bare
> and to which he forces them to direct their eyes. Let them look—I
> shall look with them, in my mind's eye. I let myself be jostled along
> in those same apathetic, or perhaps shuddering lines. Our thick-
> walled torture chamber, into which Germany was transformed by a
> vile regime of conspirators . . . has been burst open, and our ignom-
> iny lies naked before the eyes of the world.

The "transatlantic general" was George S. Patton. In the second half of this chapter, juxtaposing it with all this, the narrative returns to

> the last years of my hero's intellectual life, the two years 1929 and 1930, years of highly excited and enormous—one is tempted to say, monstrous—creative activity, a kind of tumult [ending with] his final and ultimate work: the symphonic cantata *The Lamentation of Doctor Faustus.*

All that has gone before brings together around 1930 the rise of National Socialism and Leverkühn's climactic musical statement, another "break-through," in which Leverkühn takes back the optimism of the Ninth Symphony, of Schiller, Lessing, and Goethe, but ends with a final and exiguous "hope beyond hope." Again, in Zeitblom's description of the long hour-and-a-half lament, the novel moves from language to a work which is

> properly speaking, undynamic, lacking development and without drama, in much the same way as when a stone is cast into water the concentric circles that spread farther and farther, one around the other, are without drama and always the same. A single immense variation on lamentation (and as such related to the finale of the Ninth Symphony with its variations on jubilation), it expands its rings, each inexorably drawing the others after it: movements, grand variations.

But, like the Faust of the old *Faustbook,* who says, "I die as a bad and as a good Christian," the *Lamentation,* weaving that old farewell into its text, turns back on itself. Given the disposition of thematic forces in *Doctor Faustus,* this is as if in the *Divine Comedy* the pilgrim Dante's journey through hell took 99 cantos, and then, near the end of canto 100, there occurred a sudden repentance, and then some lines of the *Purgatorio,* with the merest hint of divine grace—and then, nothing. Zeitblom's description must be quoted again:

> Just listen to the ending, listen with me: One instrumental group after the other steps back, and what remains as the work fades away in the high G of a cello, the final word, the final sound, float-ing off, slowly vanishing in a *pianissimo fermata.* Then nothing more. Silence and night. But the tone, which is no more, for which, as it hangs there vibrating in the silence, only the soul listens, and

what was the dying note of sorrow—is no longer that, its meaning changes, it stands as a light in the night.

The long lament of the cantata musically declared repentance. The love Adrian felt for the beautiful child Nepomuk and the child's terrible end, in which Adrian believes he is implicated, have broken his cold heart and borne in upon him profound awareness of what he has lost, and now remembers. The horror of his own inhumanity, his arrogance, his Faustian ambition, and his seeking out evil in the form of infection are now expressed by sound in the *Lamentation,* the only hope reverberating in that last high G—that sound followed by silence. This hope, surrounded by darkness, this "light in the night," has been anticipated by Adrian's theological and theoretical victor over the third manifestation of the devil in Penestrino: a "sinfulness so hopeless that it allows its man fundamentally to despair of hope is the true theological path to salvation." It is Pauline and Augustinian, and resembles some twentieth-century radical but orthodox Protestant theology as in Kierkegaard, the hope existing despite the emptiness, as between the Crucifixion and Easter. In his long lamentation fused with repentance, Leverkühn has found the power to move wrenchingly beyond his pact with the devil.

The tragic-comic climax of *Doctor Faustus* comes in the final chapter, followed by a brief coda describing Leverkühn's death and burial. In 1939, his mind now addled by syphilis, Leverkühn arranges a sort of parodic Last Supper at the Pfeiffering farm, promising to give the invited guests an accounting of his recent work, including his playing some passages. About thirty people arrive, characters whom we have met earlier in the novel who are still alive—a "strange aquarium of creatures," Mann called it in *The Story of a Novel*—including Schiller's grandnephew the larcenous Baron Gleichen-Russwurm, who was making his first appearance since the affair with the mouse, presumably having been in prison.

Before these uncomprehending and soon impatient guests, Leverkühn, using Lutherish German again, tries to sum up his life; he puzzles and annoys the listeners by talking about his pact with Satan, but loses his way, faltering, then tries to play parts of *The Lamentation of Doctor Faustus* on the piano. He "opened his mouth as if to sing, but from between his lips there emerged only a wail that still rings in my ears. Bending over the instrument, he spread his arms wide as if to embrace it and suddenly, as if pushed, fell sideways from his chair to the floor."

We conclude that Leverkühn has understood his art and also his self-crucified Nietzschean moment in the history of Western spirituality. His story has the capability of teaching those who understand it not to be surprised by hell, which is ever present, always waiting. He has offered something more, has, in his last work, seized against the steepest possible odds that hope beyond hope, beyond the last fading sound of the *Lamentation,* in which, on the brink of damnation there is something more.

Ten years after his abortive recital, in 1940, silent now in his dementia, Adrian dies. Among those who attend his churchyard burial there was a "muffled, unrecognizable stranger, who had vanished again as the first clods fell on the lowered coffin." This, we are certain, is the former prostitute, now Madame de Tolna, who had discovered her own worth and her spirituality through him, and had in fact married him with the Renaissance ring, its esoteric serpent-and-dart design symbolizing her knowledge of what had happened at the bordello in Pressburg.

Serenus Zeitblom has been shaken, serene no more. His "listen with me" echoes Faust's "watch with me," which itself echoes Jesus (Matthew 26:40). Zeitblom, Ph.D., has begun to recover some of the essential content of his humanism, awareness of the depth of evil and at the end of *Doctor Faustus* can speak not only for himself but to and for Germany:

> In those days [1940], Germany, a hectic flush on its cheeks, was reeling at the height of its savage triumphs, about to win the world on the strength of the one pact it intended to keep and had signed with its blood. Today [1945], in the embrace of demons, a hand over one eye, the other staring into the horror, it plummets from despair to despair. When will it reach the bottom of the abyss? When, out of this final hopelessness, will a miracle that goes beyond faith bear the light of hope? A lonely man folds his hands and says, "May God have mercy on your poor soul, my friend, my fatherland."

At the end here Zeitblom has been able to speak in truth-telling prose, no longer in hesitating equivocations as at the beginning. He has also prayed. However, an important reservation must be entered regarding *Doctor Faustus,* having to do with the drastic character of the spiritual experience represented in it. The devil(s) in those Palestrina dialogues had expressed the thought that "mediocrity has no theological standing." He meant by "mediocrity" those unprepared for, even unsuited to, Leverkühn-like spiritual agonies, or ready to undertake the journeys of Saint Augustine or the pilgrim Dante in the *Divine Comedy.* Remember that Mann does depict powerful forces coming from outside the hell of Germany and represented by that "transatlantic general" George S. Patton. Somewhere between the extremes of angel and devil there is glimpsed in that American general the decency of the ordinary man, courageous, willing, honest. That is not a modernist thought, but that general should be remembered.

It might be asked whether *Doctor Faustus,* in which the presence of Luther and the Lutheran sense of sin is so strong, does not itself, as a novel, express that kind of Lutheranism by omitting an important part of the Christian humanist tradition. Is *Doctor Faustus* not "Tertullianist," as Fritz Kaufmann sees, viewing Tertullian as the first Protestant?[13] Tertullian (circa 162–225 B.C.) fought against the incorporation of Greek language and thought into Christian understanding, asking, "What is Athens to Jerusalem?" But he lost this great argument to the ecclesiastical party of Origen and Clement of Alexandria.[14] The central humanist tradition thus held in balance Athens and Jerusalem, with Athens affirming both Eros and Agape, human love and divine love. While deeply aware of evil, man in this balance did not teeter weakly on the edge of demoniac lechery, frenzy, and the Pit. While the prefatory material of *Doctor Faustus,* using Virgil and Dante, retains the synthesis, by the end of *Doctor Faustus* we appear to be left only with Tertullian, jettisoning reason and all that it implies (General Patton, the world, the fight itself). Well, *Doctor Faustus* is Faustian. Serenus Zeitblom has been educated by Leverkühn. He can describe the music, he can comprehend the experience, and he writes this story amid the flames and stench of the Third Reich, and so its extremity, its Tertullianism, does work dramatically. And yes, today, the balance of the classical must be re-earned through an awareness of the irrational always present powerfully in man's depths. And yet Aeneas, though Troy is behind him in ashes, does kill Turnus in battle and goes on to found Rome.

Was Thomas Mann a Christian? No, not so far as we can tell; he did not believe in God and was a secular humanist. But his *novel* is Christian. What Mann hopes for here in this unquestionably great work is a reinvigorated, informed, and even learned—he certainly leads the reader in that direction—intellectually aristocratic humanism freshly possessed of the insights of its great exemplars, aware of evil, calling it by its name, and both toughened and resolute against it.

Certainly *Doctor Faustus* is a German novel, suffused with German tradition, many German master spirits present in it through allusion or implication. But this is a European novel as well, and Mann hoped for a Europeanized Germany which would replace the dark dream of a Germanized Europe. The Europeanized Germany would come, but he did not live to see it, and all of Europe knows that the history of the twentieth century cannot be allowed to happen again.

Very early in his career as a novelist, Mann said that he would probably reach the height of his powers between the ages of sixty and seventy. *Doctor Faustus* was published in 1947 when he was sixty-seven, though he had been pondering the theme at least since 1934, a suggestive date for that theme. It belongs to those of his novels that Mann, following Heine, liked to compare to a great tapestry. In view of the form of *Doctor Faustus,* the term *symphonic* could also be applied. Some have found it too cerebral; others, like Martin Greenberg, too premeditated, "Daedalian." But, as we have seen, it contains marvelous local surprises, and it does possess great energies that are felt throughout. One might call it Leverkühnian. In the demands it makes, *Doctor Faustus* is also a modernist novel, a late modernist work in the movement with foundations in the nineteenth century with Baudelaire, symbolism, and much else, and it came forward, for example, in 1899 with Conrad's *Heart of Darkness* and in 1908 with Picasso's *Demoiselles d'Avignon* (*Young Ladies of Avignon*). As Pound urged, Mann's novel itself "made it new." With Leverkühn's music and Mann's *Doctor Faustus* we have late modernism, under extreme pressure. Whether we will have a reinvigorated humanism, a humanism with knowledge, courage, and teeth, probably depends to a considerable degree on the universities, and remains very much to be seen.

Afterword

Thomas Mann's *Doctor Faustus* (1947) stands as a magisterial summation of modernism, its "high G of a cello, the last word, the last fainting sound, slowly dying in a pianissimo-fermata. Then nothing more, silence and night. But that tone, which vibrates in the silence, which is no longer there, to which only the spirit hearkens, and which was the voice of mourning, is no more. It changes its meaning; it abides as a light in the night." This remains in the mind of the reader as an example of the exigent point around which the chaos of experience could be organized. Transcending the fragmentary world of *The Waste Land*, there is Eliot's "still point," the moment in-and-out of time that Eliot called "incarnation." Frost resisted this with empiricism, his metaphorical birch tree raising him "toward heaven," but returning him to earth: because "Earth's the right place for love:/I don't know where it's likely to go better." But in his late poem "Directive," a quasi pilgrimage ended at a brook, "cold as a spring as yet so near its source,/Too lofty and original to rage," "a broken drinking goblet like the Grail . . . Drink and be whole again beyond confusion." In "The Figure a Poem Makes," Frost said that poetry can provide "a momentary stay against confusion," as in "Directive." Poetry itself for a "moment" organizes experience. That is as far as Frost's empiricism allows him to go.

Hemingway experienced versions of "the good place," but resisted fear and death with courage and resolution, as expressed in his disciplined style. Such redeeming "good places" recur, as in "Cross-Country Snow" (*In Our Time*). Nick Adams and his friend George are skiing in the Swiss Alps: "The rush and the sudden swoop as he dropped down a steep undulation plucked Nick's mind out and left him only the wonderful flying, dropping sensation in his body." The following exchange indicates that this experience means much more to Nick than to George. We already know that Nick is back from the war after being wounded:

"Maybe we'll never go skiing again, Nick," George said.
"We've got to," said Nick. "It isn't worth while if you can't."
"We'll go, all right," George said.
"We've got to," Nick agreed.

The "good place" is essential to Nick, who has been wounded and experienced near death, but it is not necessary to George.

At the end of *In Our Time,* Nick fishes in the Big Two-Hearted River, another redemptive experience. But he refuses to fish further down the river in the difficult swamp. It would be *tragic,* he says. The "good place" must be perfect. Another good place appears in chapter 12 of *The Sun Also Rises* when Jake and Bill fish idyllically at Burguete, up in the high ground of Basque Country. The good place always involves a simplification of ordinary life. In *A Farewell to Arms* Frederic Henry finds security and for a while companionship with Catherine, but we finally understand that death is outside his window and at the end he walks alone outside in the rain.

For Fitzgerald there is the "green light" of possibility, while over the "wasteland" there always rises the Gatsbyan moon of romance.

Beginning in Paris during the 1880s, modernism addressed the exigencies of a broken world and not only produced many masterpieces that will endure, but made discoveries of permanent value. Marilynne Robinson's *Gilead,* published in 2004, is a late modernist novel, its narrator, the Reverend John Ames, a native-born Heideggerian in his perception of the weight of Being, the *isness* that all individual existences share:

> We participate in Being without remainder. No breath, no thought, no wart or whisker, is not as sunk in Being as it could be. And yet no one can say what Being is. If you describe what a thought and a whisker have in common, and a typhoon and a rise in the stock market, excluding "existence," which merely restates the fact that they have a place on our list of known and nameable things . . .

Yet we—like the Reverend Ames—sense that there is more, a weight that is more than that of individual existences. We are surprised that the Reverend John Ames was born in Gilead, Iowa, and not in Messkirch, Germany.

In fact, modernism, though revolutionary in its time, is also traditional in that it takes its place in the search for a principle of order that goes back to the pre-Socratics and then to Socrates himself, as presented by Plato. We see in the Gospel of John an appropriation of Greek philosophy when it sees Jesus as the *Logos*. In the long history of culture, from the pre-Socratics and extending into the future, there will occur periods when the existing culture tends to lose its legitimacy, as happened during the nineteenth century. Then, as Eliot looked back to Dante and Donne, we will look back to the modernists.

But the journey will continue into the future, as writers continue to give shape and meaning to experience.

Fare forward, Voyager . . .

Chapter One
Robert Frost and T. S. Eliot: Modernisms

1. Matthew Spencer, ed., *Elected Friends: Robert Frost and Edward Thomas to One Another* (New York: Handsel, 2003).

2. Pound's reviews of Frost are collected in *The Literary Essays of Ezra Pound,* edited and introduced by T. S. Eliot (New York: New Directions, 1968).

3. Spencer, *Elected Friends,* 207–9.

4. Ibid., 129–30.

5. Cited in B. C. Southam, *A Guide to the Selected Poems of T. S. Eliot* (New York: Harcourt, Brace and World, 1969), 71–72.

6. Lawrence Rainey, ed., *The Annotated Waste Land with Eliot's Contemporary Prose* (New Haven: Yale University Press, 2005), 34–35.

7. Robert Frost, *Selected Letters of Robert Frost,* ed. Lawrence Thompson (New York: Holt, Rinehart and Winston, 1964), 52.

8. Donald Hall, "Robert Frost Corrupted," *Atlantic Monthly,* March 1982. Mr. Hall analyzes many examples of how Edward Connery Lathem, editor of this edition, corrupted the text of Frost's poems by adding commas and other punctuation.

9. A tape recording of this occasion is available in Rauner Library Special Collections at Dartmouth College. Jay Parini transcribes part of Eliot's remarks in *Robert Frost: A Life* (New York: Holt, 1999), 402–3.

Chapter Two
F. Scott Fitzgerald: A Capacity for Wonder

1. Lionel Trilling, "Fitzgerald Plain," in *Speaking of Literature and Society,* ed. Diana Trilling (New York: Harcourt, Brace, Jovanovich, 1980), 258.

2. Ibid, 259.

3. F. Scott Fitzgerald, "Princeton," in *Afternoon of an Author* (New York: Scribner's, 1957).

4. James L. W. West III, *The Perfect Hour: The Romance of F. Scott Fitzgerald and Ginevra King, His First Love* (New York: Random House, 2005). Using letters and diaries, West provides a very good account of this relationship and also a close look at the dating and courtship manners of the period.

5. Lionel Trilling, "Scott Fitzgerald," in *The Liberal Imagination: Essays on Literature and Society* (New York: Viking Press, 1950), 250.

6. Jeffrey Hart, "Faust in Great Neck," in *Smiling Through the Cultural Catastrophe: Toward the Revival of Higher Education* (New Haven: Yale University Press, 2001).

7. John Davies, *The Legend of Hobey Baker* (Boston: Little, Brown, 1966). This provides a good account of an important figure of the time, who was the epitome of the gentleman athlete. Of considerable charm and interest is Mark Goodman's novel *Hurrah for the Next Man Who Dies* (New York: Atheneum, 1985). Hobey Baker is the hero of this novel, and Mr. Goodman has a remarkable ability to portray the man and his time. Like many good novels, this has largely been forgotten, but should be reissued.

8. Among the stories inspired by Ginevra King, Mr. West lists "The Jelly-Bean" (1920), "Winter Dreams" (1922), "Dice, Brassknuckles and Guitar" (1923), "Diamond Dick and the First Law of Woman" (1924), "The Third Casket" (1924), "The Unspeakable Egg" (1924), "John Jackson's Arcady" (1924), "Love in the Night" (1925), "Not in the Guide Book" (1925), "A Penny Spent" (1926), "Presumption" (1926), "The Adolescent Marriage" (1926), "The Love Boat" (1927), "Flight and Pursuit" (1932), "The Rubber Check" (1932), "More Than Just a House" (1933), and "New Types" (1934). Most of Fitzgerald's income after *This Side of Paradise* came from short stories written for magazines, and most of those listed above were relatively inaccessible until the publication of *The Price Was High: Fifty Uncollected Stories,* ed. Matthew J. Bruccoli (New York: MJF Books, 1979).

9. Matthew Bruccoli, introductory note to "The Rich Boy," in *The Short Stories of F. Scott Fitzgerald* (New York: Scribner's, 1989), 397.

10. Matthew Bruccoli, conversation with the author at the Century Association in Manhattan, 2001.

Chapter Three
Hemingway, Fitzgerald, and *The Sun Also Rises*
1. We know that Hemingway and Fitzgerald discussed Michael Arlen's novels at least once. See Carlos Baker, *Ernest Hemingway: A Life Story* (New York: Scribner's, 1969), 146. For Fitzgerald's mention of *The Green Hat,* see "Echoes of the Jazz Age," in *The Crack-Up,* ed. Edmund Wilson (New York: J. Laughlin, 1945), 17.

Chapter Four
Hemingway's Best Novel
1. Hemingway, nineteen, fell in love with Agnes von Kurowsky, a nurse he met in Milan in 1918 after being wounded at Fossalta. His memory of his love for her contributed to *A Farewell to Arms.* Hemingway's biographers occasionally have been tempted to take as autobiography what he wrote as fiction. In his 1969 biography of Hemingway, Carlos Baker bases his account of Hemingway's wound on the details of Frederic Henry's wound, and Kenneth Lynn, writing about sex between Frederic and Catherine in the Milan hospital and in considering Hemingway's plaster cast, speculates about the sexual positions Hemingway and Agnes might have used. James Nagel and Henry Serrano Villard have provided a factual and curiously haunting account of Hemingway and von Kurowsky's relationship, *Hemingway in Love and War* (Boston: Northeastern University Press, 1989). This study uses her diary and

letters along with other primary material to demonstrate that a sexual relationship between Hemingway and Agnes was almost certainly out of the question. She was seven years older than Hemingway and in her letters addressed him as "Kid." The Red Cross Hospital in Milan had open links between rooms with cooling wind blowing through and little chance of privacy. She had been born in Germantown, Pennsylvania, on January 3, 1892, her father a naturalized American citizen from Königsberg. Until sailing for Europe on the *La Lorraine,* she had led a relatively sheltered life, only then becoming aware of her attractiveness to men and enjoying some flirtations. There is no doubt, based on her diary and letters, that she was genuinely attracted to Hemingway and affectionate in her letters. But she was also critical in her letters of behavior among nurses that she considered to go beyond the bounds of propriety. In her letters to Hemingway she seems to have told him what she knew he would like to hear. She continued to see other men and tell Hemingway about them. On March 7, 1919, she wrote to him in Oak Park, ending any thought of marriage: "I somehow feel that some day I'll have reason to be proud of you." Hemingway never forgot his rejection, resembling Scott Fitzgerald after his rejection by Ginevra King. Fitzgerald repeatedly used Ginevra in his fiction. Hemingway, in contrast, hit back at Agnes in "A Very Short Story," which appears in *In Our Time,* where he changes "Ag" to "Luz." Hemingway used his fantasy romance with Agnes in *A Farewell to Arms,* but based Catherine on his first wife, Hadley Richardson.

Hemingway in Love provides valuable background information about that period, not only about Agnes von Kurowsky and Hemingway, but also about the Norton-Harjes Red Cross ambulance service in 1918, an elite group with many volunteers from Harvard. Its founder, Richard Norton, was the son of Harvard president Charles Eliot Norton, and it was virtually a literary movement, including Hemingway and also John Dos Passos, E. E. Cummings, Harry Crosby, Louis Bromfield, and Dashiell Hammett; Henry James was one of the many who contributed to its support. When they enlisted, all were idealists.

2. Valerie Hemingway, *Running with the Bulls: My Years with the Hemingways* (New York: Ballantine, 2004). Valerie Denby-Smith, born in Dublin, worked for Hemingway as a secretary and accompanied him on his trip to Spain in 1959 when he followed the mano-a-mano series of corridas between Ordóñez and Dominguín that was published in "The Dangerous Summer," commissioned as a 10,000-word article for *Life.* That summer proved to be dangerous not only to the toreros but also to Hemingway—his excessive eating and drinking and his increasingly evident signs of mental illness, including fantasies of persecution by the IRS and threats of suicide.

3. Lionel Trilling, "An American in Spain" (1941), in *Speaking of Literature and Society,* ed. Diana Trilling (New York: Harcourt Brace Jovanovich, 1980), 170.

4. The most extensive treatment of Hemingway and the antifascist popular front is Stephen Koch's *The Breaking Point: Hemingway, Dos Passos, and the Murder of José Robles* (New York: Counterpoint, 2005). Robles, a lieutenant

colonel in the Loyalist army and a prominent antifascist, was murdered by Stalin's agents when Moscow abandoned its antifascism and looked toward an understanding with Hitler. Hemingway was crushed, he even wept, when he saw the International Brigades marching out of Spain north through Barcelona toward France. Hemingway's icy indifference to the murder of José Robles, a friend of Dos Passos's, destroyed their friendship. Hemingway's own disillusion with the Communists in Spain becomes clear in *For Whom the Bell Tolls* (1940). We see the power of the Stalinists at Gaylord's Hotel in Madrid, and the near insanity of André Marty, Stalinist commissar of the International Brigades. Despite all this, *For Whom the Bell Tolls* unambiguously supports the Loyalist cause, and the hero Robert Jordan dies in the antifascist cause.

5. Ernest Hemingway, *The Dangerous Summer* (New York: Scribner's, 1985).

6. V. Hemingway, *Running with the Bulls,* 97–98.

7. Posthumously published Hemingway novels show none of the discipline characteristic of his work through 1929. *Islands in the Stream* (1970) is a long rambling conventional novel. *The Garden of Eden* (1986) could be said to have been manufactured out of a long manuscript and can hardly be said to be a novel "by Ernest Hemingway."

8. See also Jacqueline Tavernier-Courbin, *Ernest Hemingway's "A Moveable Feast": The Making of Myth* (Boston: Northeastern University Press, 1991). This casts doubt on the importance and even the existence of the documents supposedly contained in a trunk kept in storage at the Ritz Hotel in Paris since 1927, and shows how extensively Mary Hemingway edited the text, amounting to more than editing ordinarily involves but stopping short of rewriting. This argument does not account for the concise quality of these sketches.

9. Professor Louis Renza, conversation with the author, March 2006.

Chapter Five
Gilead: A Rumor of Angels

1. Peter Berger, *A Rumor of Angels* (New York: Doubleday/Anchor, 1990), 179.

2. James Wood, *New York Times Book Review,* November 28, 2004, 1.

3. Joan Acocella, "A Note of the Miraculous," *New York Review of Books,* July 9, 2005, 14–18.

4. Rüdiger Safranski, *Martin Heidegger: Between Good and Evil,* trans. Ewald Osers (Cambridge, Mass.: Harvard University Press, 1998). Safranski is especially useful in connecting Heidegger's "moment of vision" with analogous phenomena central to the thought of Carl Schmitt's *kairos,* Kierkegaard's "moment" when God bursts into his life and the individual feels summoned to risk the leap into faith: "At such a moment the historical time that separates the individual from Christ loses its significance" (173). To this should be added Eliot's "still point," the "moment in and out of time" that he called "incarnation." (Safranski provides a brief account of the 1929 debate at Davos between Heidegger and Cassirer. Cassirer was a philosopher in the idealist tradition, Heidegger the enemy of abstraction. A major cultural event, this was widely compared with the debate between Settembrini and Naphta in Mann's *Magic Mountain.*)

5. What the Reverend John Ames says here is sound. Had he not sensed Jack's lack of seriousness, indeed hostility, he might have added that our hearts are predestined to sin, but that God in his love, mercy, and sovereignty is far greater than our hearts and can conquer the sinfulness of our bent wills. Calvin says that because God's will is not bound by our human concepts, we know that he is a God of love and can hope that he will save all his creatures. In 2006 Marilynne Robinson provided a preface to *Steward of God's Covenant: Selected Writings,* ed. John F. Thornton (New York: Vintage, 2006). She writes authoritatively about John Calvin.

6. Acocella, "Note of the Miraculous." Joan Acocella, as well as writing on dance for the *New Yorker,* has written excellent literary criticism in *Willa Cather and the Politics of Criticism* (Lincoln: University of Nebraska Press, 2000).

7. *New Yorker,* November 21, 2005, 100–101. See also Marco Grassi, "The Angelic Friar," *New Criterion,* December 2005, 23–27. He notices the "brilliance and translucence that Fra Angelico obtained by applying the palest of glazes over a bright, almost opalescent preparatory layer."

Chapter Six
Mann's *Doctor Faustus:* The Moment in the Depths of Silence

1. Marguerite Yourcenar, "Humanism in Thomas Mann," in *The Partisan Review Anthology,* ed. William Phillips and Philip Rahv (New York: Holt, Rinehart and Winston, 1962), 185–202.

2. F. W. Dupee, *"The King of the Cats," and Other Remarks on Writers and Writing* (New York: Farrar, Straus and Giroux, 1965).

3. Thomas Mann, *The Story of a Novel: The Genesis of Doctor Faustus,* trans. Richard and Clara Winston (New York: Knopf, 1961), 220.

4. John Banville, *New York Times Book Review,* November 17, 2002.

5. Mann, *Story of a Novel,* 64.

6. Curtis Cate, *Friedrich Nietzsche* (London: Hutchinson, 2002). On page seventy-two of this generally admirable and well-documented biography, Cate deals with the matter of Nietzsche's visit(s) to a brothel: "Nietzsche, after his first frightening glimpse of such an establishment in Cologne, seems to have returned more resolutely to the attack. There is even reason to believe that he contracted syphilis and had to make several visits to a Leipzig doctor, to be cured of this humiliating ailment. There is here a mystery that will probably never be elucidated, but which helps to explain Nietzsche's later mental breakdown in his forty-fourth year." Cate appears to be unaware of Nietzsche's 1865 letter to Paul Deussen, with its vivid account of his brothel visit. This is odd because Mann discusses this letter in his 1947 essay "Nietzsche's Philosophy in the Light of Recent History."

7. Fritz Kaufmann, *Thomas Mann: The World as Will and Representation* (Boston: Beacon Press, 1957).

8. Ibid., 199.

9. *The Story of a Novel* goes into considerable detail about Mann's debt to Theodor Adorno for the musical theory in *Doctor Faustus,* especially Adorno's *Philosophy of Modern Music.* Mann also includes a postscript to the novel in

which he acknowledges the example of Arnold Schoenberg's twelve-tone scale. Those influences certainly are important for Leverkühn's music, but the shape of Leverkühn's life reflects the example of Nietzsche.

10. Rainey, *Annotated Waste Land*, 33.

11. For a more detailed discussion, see Victor A. Oswald Jr., "Thomas Mann's *Doktor Faustus:* The Enigma of Frau von Tolna," *Germanic Review* 13 (1948): 249–53. Mr. Oswald valuably explores linguistic clues placed in the narrative by Mann.

12. Mann, *Story of a Novel*, 217–18.

13. Kaufmann, *Thomas Mann*, 202.

14. Hart, *Cultural Catastrophe*, 6–11, explores the struggle of Clement and Origen versus Tertullian, and locates it in the larger story of Western civilization. During the second half of the third century, Clement of Alexandria and Origen argued that though the Greek poets and philosophers did not possess the revelations of Christianity, they were not inherently good or bad and could be useful to Christianity. Tertullian disagreed.

SELECTED WORKS

T. S. Eliot. *The Waste Land and Other Poems*. London: Faber and Faber, 1940.

Robert Frost. *Collected Poems of Robert Frost*. New York: Henry Holt and Company, 1930.

F. Scott Fitzgerald. *The Great Gatsby*. New York: Charles Scribner's Sons, 1925.

———. *This Side of Paradise*. New York: Charles Scribner's Sons, 1920.

Ernest Hemingway. *A Farewell to Arms*. New York: Charles Scribner's Sons, 1929.

———. *in our time*. Pamphlet. Paris: Three Mountains Press, 1924.

———. *In Our Time*. New York: Boni and Liveright, 1925.

———. *The Sun Also Rises*. New York: Charles Scribner's Sons, 1926.

Marilynne Robinson. *Gilead*. New York: Farrar, Straus and Giroux, 2004.

Thomas Mann. *Doctor Faustus: The Life of the German Composer Adrian Leverkühn As Told by a Friend*. Translated from the German by John E. Woods. New York: Alfred A. Knopf, 1997.

809.9112 HART
Hart, Jeffrey Peter
The living moment :
   modernism in a broken
   world

R0120117674   SDY_SP

DISCARD

OCT   2012

SANDY SPRINGS

Atlanta-Fulton Public Library